The Sitt

Irene Watson

Plain View Press
P. O. 42255
Austin, TX 78704

plainviewpress.net
sbright1@austin.rr.com
1-512-441-2452

Copyright 2005, Irene Watson. All rights reserved.
ISBN: 1-891386-49-2
Library of Congress Number: 2005907307

Cover art, *Holding Happiness* by Austin, TX artist, Kay Martin.
www.kaymartin.com

Irene's photo by LeRoy Lawson.

Forward

In over twenty-five years of clinical practice as a psychologist I have had the privilege of listening to clients tell thier stories in order to arrive at the truth. Through telling our story each of us learns to sort out appearances from reality, our *persona* or false self from our true identity. It is in storytelling that we uncover the true meanings of the metaphors that our lives have pieced together in a sort of hieroglyphic code of human events, joys and sorrows, laughter and pain, beauty and despair. Regardless of an individual's station in life, their accomplishments, talent or circumstances, I have never met a person who does not benefit from help with the transformation of their story into a spiritual masterpiece that gives life meaning.

The Sitting Swing is a living metaphor in which Irene Watson generously and artfully invites the reader to experience the stories of her life in order to decode their own. We are drawn in by the unassuming and magnetic quality of the narrative, as she reflects on life and all its irritations and grandeur from perspectives of humility and curiosity that welcome us with candor. She includes us in her own struggles with self-knowledge from inside the halls of "Avalon," a cleverly camouflaged treatment center where I myself consulted for several years.

I confess that I couldn't help scouring each page for a hint of preachiness or moralism that seemed inevitable. Certainly none of us would tolerate another condescending lecture on how to live better lives. Frankly, it was to my true surprise that I found myself appreciating it even more after the third read, than the first. Apparently it is true – "Seek the Truth and the Truth Shall Set You Free " – free even from evangelizing. In *The Sitting Swing*, Irene Watson gives us a powerful glimpse inside a treatment center where the characters are just as real and flawed as we are. She exposes the myth that addictions are about drugs and alcohol and helps us both love and laugh at ourselves in a spirit of wisdom and humanity.

Since graduate school in psychology, I have been especially fond of the notion that we are all spiritual beings going through a human experience. I reject the fiction that mental health practitioners are perfected and anointed beings charged with the task of healing others. In fact, my favorite definition of psychology is "the care of the Id by the odd" and one of my favorite books on the subject is "The Myth of Mental Illness." I embrace the belief that we are all being called out of our collective and consensual cultural trances to awaken to our real purpose for being. While societies may lend themselves to stereotyping and marginalizing certain behaviors and attributes as "normal" and "crazy," I am drawn by the metaphysical writers who challenge us to think above our thinking to the real truth about life and its purpose.

In *The Sitting Swing*, Irene Watson tells her tale and lets the reader do the translating. She allows us to insert ourselves into the story and decode the enigmas of our own lives.

Jan Ford Mustin, Ph.D.
Clinical psychologist and author of *Removing Your Roadblocks to Love, Happiness and Success*

Acknowledgements

I was inspired to write this book after reading two memoirs, *Change Me Into Zeus's Daughter* by Barbara Robinette Moss and *Lost and Found* by Babette Hughes. Their stories about healing their childhood wounds and reclaiming their true self gave me the push I needed to write my story with hope that it will inspire others to make changes in their lives.

To write a book about my childhood was very cathartic on one hand, yet very frightening on the other. During my writing I felt detached from the little girl whom I was writing about, yet there were many times I was reliving the past. I would have never finished the book if I didn't have loving support from my friends and family during this time. I acknowledge with much gratitude:

My readers while I was writing this narrative chapter by chapter. I appreciate their encouragement to continue writing until the book was completed.

The two *Goddesses* in my life, Jean Carpenter Backus and Lisa McCurley. They not only supported me throughout the writing and publishing of this book, but they acknowledge of who I really am and all that happens is in divine order. My long time friend and soul sister, Florence Gore. She's always here for me, even from a distance.

My Master Mind partners, Stan Biderman, Sheryl Draker and Mel Waxler. Their weekly support for 12 years was one of the most stable things in my life. They saw for me what I couldn't see, they believed for me what I couldn't believe and they encouraged me to grow.

The influential characters in this book, Margie, Jean, Jorge and Nichole. They saw past the façade I created for self-protection and encouraged me to remove the shield and expose who I really am.

Susan Bright from Plain View Press for publishing this book. Without her, my story would still be a manuscript! Jill Mayfield for believing my story is worth reading. Christine Watson, my daughter-in-law, and Eileen Urschell for their diligent proof reading.

Alexander. Without his birth my life may have been different. Or, maybe not. My parents for bringing me into this world to experience and learn the path to find my true self.

My husband Bob for being patient with me as I was trekking on a path to find out who I really am. For his loving encouragement and support in all my dreams, small and large. To our children, Juanita and Daryn, whom I have encouraged to re-write the script. They no longer have to follow a script that has been in place for many generations.

Dedicated to
You,
the reader.

This narrative, according to my memory and perception, is of my life and how I found a way to find peace within. May reading it help you find your own true self.

The names of some people and descriptions have been changed to preserve anonymity.

Gifts

How can those waves be so calming
as they churn, whip and wind,
roaring, howling, tormenting the sea life,
washing ashore helpless jellyfish?

And yet,
as I gaze into the vastness
I realize that every wave portrays life's thoughts,
churning, whipping and winding.
tormenting my own life,
leaving me in a feeling of helplessness.

Sadness overcomes me.
Tears well in my eyes.

The wave breaks, smoothes out, and gently rolls
unto the shore.
It slides back softly
leaving behind ripples in the sand
and gifts of sea shells and coral.
I too break away from torment,
and quietly accept the gifts.

                Irene Watson

Chapter One

It was the damndest thing that they thought I'd fall for it. A video camera in plain site, one corner of my room, pointing right in on everything I'd be doing for the next twenty eight days. Not likely. I couldn't figure why they wouldn't bother hiding the thing. Even a hanging plant in front might have kept me from noticing for an hour or two. But they didn't even try, and that was their real weakness as far as I was concerned. Here they were, helping some of the most messed-up people you can imagine, people addicted to just about anything, and they thought these people would just reveal everything about themselves in an instant? That they would have cameras watching them get dressed, watching them sleep?

Some experts. I started to wonder why I'd paid good money to be here. But there it is – we all want to fit in. I had too many friends graduate from this utopian little institute, and they all swore it changed their lives. They all used "Avalon talk" as I called it – the catch phrases and jargon used in this Avalon Center. Tiring as it was to listen to their new language, they were my friends, and it was even more of a challenge to be outside the group in that way. So, I decided to call some of my own challenges "addictions" and to make a trip here. Twenty eight days of dealing with real addicts, then I could graduate and get back on the inside track with my friends.

I pulled a chair out from the small desk in my room and turned it to face the camera, then sat and reclined myself a bit against its stiff back. I folded my arms across my chest and looked with a cold grit at the camera. I probably looked the way my own kids did when they decided to pull the rebel thing. It's not that I was overly confrontational, but a camera was a statement, and I would make one right back. I stared it down, just hoping that someone was watching me live. I wanted my eyes to tell the story – you might have me stuck here, you might control a lot of what I do, and I might even tell you a thing or two about myself, but you're not invading my privacy. There was a me that I would share.

After a three-minute stare down, I got up from my seat and rummaged through my suitcase, pulling out a white washcloth. That would do the trick. I walked to the camera and flipped the cloth up over top of the thing, covering its lens. I brushed my hands against each other in mocking way. Done and done, I thought.

The camera wasn't the only reason I felt this place was like a prison. For starters, you weren't allowed to bring books, magazines, tapes, a radio. No incoming phone calls either. They pretty much had your input covered. From then on, you'd get input from them or from your own brain, and that was

11

about it. And that still wasn't it for the prison atmosphere. Everything I'd need for those twenty eight days, I had to bring with me – clothes, toiletries, extra money. Well, they *did* offer things like massages, so cash wasn't a bad idea. But isn't that a little like pleasantries to keep shackled people happy? Amazing that I'd heard nothing but good things about the place from my friends. Most of these points I knew ahead of time, but the camera had put me on edge. Maybe the big joke among graduates was to get other people to attend so they'd experience a month of prison too, sort of a hazing ceremony to get back inside with your friends. Looking around myself, that didn't seem out of the question.

The place was called "Avalon" with good reason. Well, it wasn't so glorious as the island from the Arthurian legends, where magic was supposed to reside and where Arthur himself was said to be healed of a mortal wound. But the place was on an island, relatively hidden from the world, connected to the mainland only by a long and narrow bridge. Maybe half a mile from the center, there was a very small resort community, resident population five hundred year 'round, and twice that in the summertime. It wasn't what you'd call a booming tourist destination, but it had its visitors. A road circling the island connected the community, the Center, and substantial woods covering the area.

Those woods and this room seemed the only real havens, now that the camera was out of the loop, where I would have some time to myself. The rest of Avalon was made up of common rooms where groups would gather either for recreation or for talking sessions led by the staff here. Those were the sessions, I'd been told, when people learned what it meant to open themselves up in front of a bunch of other addicts. And if scrutiny from other addicts wasn't bad enough, that's when the staff would direct you to confront all your issues. I wasn't one to avoid issues, but there are two facts about that. First, you don't deal with that stuff in front of other people. On that point I was sure. The last thing someone needs on their path to healing is to have a bunch of others judging them. Second, I had some disappointments about my life so far. But I doubted that *any* of my challenges really counted as issues, not things that had to be "fixed" by a professional anyway. Pain about some choices I'd made? Yes. A bit of insecurity about who I was? Yes. I wanted to spend time thinking about these and setting new goals. Surely new goals would help point to the "real me," as my friends now put it. But I just couldn't see how these could be "fixed" with therapy. After all, a little pain and a little insecurity didn't make me broken.

I sighed a deep sigh. Like it or not, I was here now, and I had paid to be here. Twenty eight days. I had better settle in as best I could, so I started to unpack. As I opened my few drawers and started setting in my clothes, I thought about the airport where I'd arrived. At a small bar near the luggage, I had met many of my fellow "addicts" as we waited for our ride to the Center, and I watched in disbelief as many of them chugged down drinks. I said a silent prayer of thanks that, if I had to be surrounded by addicts, at least I wasn't one for real. I felt sorry for them, but was grateful not to be among their ranks.

There were kids here in their twenties, and elders in their seventies – people up and down the scale who had seen something wrong with life as it was and wanted it fixed. There was something positive about that, and as much as I pitied most of them, I also had a small sense of hope. As I finished unpacking my clothes, I smiled with that in mind.

And then I looked up to see a woman staring into my room from the bathroom, toothbrush still in her mouth. I sighed again. Forty eight years old and I was sharing a bathroom with a perfect stranger who seemed interested to spy on me. I say "spy" because she wasn't looking at me. She was looking at the washcloth over the camera. I pretended not to notice what she was looking at, and she walked back to spit out some toothpaste. When I knew she was finished, I went in to introduce myself. "Irene Watson," I said, hand out for her to shake.

She took my hand but looked sort of absently past my shoulder. "What's that rag doing up there?"

I shrugged. "A little privacy never bothered anyone, don't you think?"

She blinked, then looked at me maybe for the first time. "Sure." She wandered back to her bedroom, and I didn't learn till later that her name was Gabby, Gabriella in fact. A native Puerto Rican living now in Connecticut, she went by Gabby, and later, I decided it was a good name for her.

Yes, things were off to a terrific start. My best course of action was becoming clearer all the time. Give them some things about me to play with, to feel that they could fix. Show how happy I was to have my problems resolved, and what I different person I could be at graduation. That way I wouldn't be opening up to people like Gabby, or to people who would put cameras in my room. And along the way, I could make use of the retreat – open up, perhaps, and spend time in personal reflection. Then at graduation, maybe I really would be different. They could let me go, believing that they'd made a difference, and I would leave, knowing that I had made a difference on my own.

But that's not how it worked at all.

Chapter Two

That evening, things began with a storm. Not the weather kind, but of the speech variety. Jorge was the director of Avalon, and he was there to make sure we understood his message clearly. "It's not that you chose it, and it's not that you want it. Fact is, I can't see any healthy person wishing it on anyone else. And here you are, clinging to it because that is your view of life."

Jorge paced back and forth at the front of the room, animated and obviously a zealot on the topic. He must have been in recovery himself. "You see, it doesn't really matter why you're here, or you're here, or you're here," he said, dangling a long finger out toward members of the crowd before him. "Because what you think of as your problem is just a symptom. That's all. The problem, my friends, is why you face these symptoms."

I started to snicker in my seat, but a look from one of the counselors standing along the wall silenced me. I couldn't help it if I started thinking of Jorge as a preacher, and I sure as heck couldn't help what I remembered of churches and sermons. But I gritted my teeth and kept quiet while he continued.

"I've got a little story for you friends." He stroked his chin a minute, as if he'd never told the story before and had to find just the right words for it. But I knew it was well-rehearsed. "I struggled through addictions myself, and I'm not even going to tell you what kinds. And you know why now, don't you? Because the kinds don't matter. The question is, why was I dealing with them?"

He paused dramatically, looking across us all. It was like those awkward moments in school when a teacher asks a question so stupid that no one wants to answer, but the teacher is looking for someone to answer anyway. Luckily none of us had to raise a hand. Jorge spelled it out. Literally. "P.A.I.N. That's right, pain, my friends. It's something everyone suffers in one form or another. And I'm here to tell you something right now, something that had better make you realize you're not alone in the world. If everyone suffers pain, then we all suffer addictions of one kind or another. Anyone who hasn't dealt with it and says he doesn't have an addiction is either lying or deceived. And sometimes, I admit, addictions aren't very obvious. But we all have forms of escape. We all have forms of getting away from whatever causes us pain. And that's what we have among this group, is it not? Forms of escape that can be overcome by simply dealing with that pain."

I loved that he said "Is it not?" It made him even more like some evangelical preacher on TV, and I got a kick out of that. Sure, for forty eight years old, I had a pretty immature sense of humor. But then again, I liked being so easily amused.

Jorge stopped pacing, stepped up a little closer to us, and lowered his voice. "But that's the challenge now, isn't it?" The atmosphere became intimate. "We've got to find that pain, find out why there is this deep need, this longing, to slip into addiction. What is your experience? Why does addiction bring you so much relief, even pleasure? These," his voice broke just a little. Oh, he was good, "these are private questions, aren't they? Questions you could never answer out loud. Questions that shouldn't even be asked!"

He glanced around. I think he was waiting for us to nod our heads when obviously we were supposed to shake them. I imagined myself standing up in a drama and calling out, "Questions we've *got* to ask, Brother! I see the light now, and I'm ready to tell it all to you. Let me face my fears, Brother! Let me *ease* the pain." I had to bite my tongue hard enough that it hurt, just to keep from laughing again. Yeah, I was easily amused.

"Co-dependence," he said after his very long pause. "Do you do whatever it takes to please those around you, even to the point of ignoring your own needs? Or does your spouse do this to keep you happy, to help smooth over the fact of your addiction? I know because I have been there. I could look directly in the eye of every person in this room and ask, 'Who, in your life, is co-dependent?' And you would have an answer for me. Maybe it is you, maybe it is your friends and family in response to you.

"If someone gives up his or her own needs to always satisfy the needs of others, this is co-dependence. And I'm not talking about giving up the things you want. I'm talking about what you need for your own well-being. Give that up because of someone else, everyone else, anyone else, there is co-dependence. It walks hand-in-hand with addiction because addictions need to be smoothed over, yes.

"But my friends," One last dramatic pause. "my friends, co-dependence is an addiction as well. It results from pain, as any addiction. And so again I say to you, we have to release that pain. That is what these twenty eight days are for. But that cannot happen without you, without you understanding that the only way to let go is to know what you must let go. The only way to be free is to know what you must escape.

"The people around you, they are in pain as you are. They are here to find freedom as you are. There is no reason to judge, and no reason to feel that you are being judged. We will speak frankly in our sessions here, because we're here to find the truth, to find the *real you* that is buried beneath the pain. I speak from experience here. You will never feel a greater release, a greater uplifting, than when you find and let go of that pain. Let's work together to achieve exactly that."

As he concluded his words, there was a hesitant applause among the crowd – maybe because they weren't sure whether they were supposed to clap in this setting. I know why I didn't clap myself. I didn't clap because something he said was true, and because after snickering about the preacher-man-addict, I wasn't laughing at the end.

I knew what co-dependence was. I had sort of diagnosed myself with it from time to time when I was frustrated, feeling buried by other people's needs. But I'd never really taken it too seriously, and I'd never thought of it as an addiction.

But why did I act that way? Was there really some pain involved that drove this in me? And most important of all, would I *ever* consider talking about pain with a group of perfect strangers? Even now I doubted it, but for the first time, that door of possibility opened up just a crack.

As I pondered all this, I watched as a counselor walked up to Jorge and pulled him to one side, whispering some matter or another to the director. Then Jorge turned to us with a serious expression on his face, with an obvious and deep concern. "I've just received some rather disappointing news, friends. But I guess it underlines my message. Here, where we need an atmosphere of real openness, someone is paranoid that we're watching you with cameras. I tell you now, it would be totally against the law for us to do so. I hope you will reconsider where you are, and what we're here for."

And with that, my door of possibility slammed shut. No way I was telling them a thing. And no way I was taking that washcloth off the camera.

Chapter Three

That intro speech by Mr. Numero Uno of Avalon was enough to tell me that away from the center was the place to be. Anywhere, as long as it was away. So early the next morning with the air still crisp, I set out around the lake, and if I somehow missed a session, well … that's how it would be. I would just play dumb.

September in Quebec, the leaves are brilliant, and in this setting they were probably every color that leaves will turn. Walking beneath the trees under those warming, almost flaming hues, would've set me at complete ease, would've made me feel like I was sitting next to a cozy fire in my home. Except for my company. There wasn't any.

I am normally all for being alone. Time to think on things. Time to breathe, relax, and not have to be anything but what I feel inside. But in this new environment, part of me wanted to have someone along, probably so I'd know I had one person to turn to during those twenty eight days. I knew from bitter experience cliques formed early, and if you didn't find your way into one, you were out for as long as things went on. So far from home, I didn't think that would feel very good. So I had asked a few of the guys that morning. Yeah, the guys. Women were right out because I also knew by experience that women were damn hard to trust. But breakfast appealed more to the guys, and I was out on my own.

I quickly learned that, for a first day anyway, this time alone couldn't have been more critical. I had been wrestling with things. Nothing that had to do with Avalon really, but things that needed sorting out in my life. And as I'd wrestled, at home, increasingly in the last few years, and during the trip here, countless images and ideas flashed through my mind about what was out of place and why it was out of place. It struck me that you couldn't really find a solution to your problems until you knew both of those points, and yet I'd never really been able to pin them down.

I knew there were some grave frustrations about my life at home because I'd never had the green light to pursue a career that would fulfill my purpose in this world. Yes, I'd had jobs that spanned many fields. But to really take a step out and do what I was supposed to do meant taking certain risks – risks I'd never had the green light to pursue. "We've got a house to pay for and take care of," said my husband. "We've got kids to raise. We've got school to pay for. We've got too many things going on. Who knows if my job is secure?" It was the kind of list you knew would never dry up, because there's always another excuse. I hated excuses. And there's nothing worse than feeling your purpose and not being able to pursue it because of them.

Granted, I didn't know quite what my purpose *was*. Not in practical terms. But I *felt* it. I knew it involved teaching of some sort. I knew it involved spirituality too. Promoting spirituality would have an important place. Not organized religion, mind you. But spirituality was a different thing, and something I knew was critical for the world.

So maybe I needed to hone those details. But first things first. Why did I come to Avalon? I wanted to learn how to use the bizarre language my friends came back from here using. I wanted to understand what was wrong in my home life and how to fix it. The way I figured it, I could listen enough during the sessions to pick up the jargon. Then on long walks and by journaling, I could gain some perspective about my life. That's what these twenty eight days were about. Time to reflect. And if no one wanted to come walking with me this morning, that was fine. If I'd found the right person to walk with, I could have spoken a lot, gotten a lot off my chest and learned in the process. But if I was alone, I would talk with the trees and grasses and squirrels. Nature would give me the answers I was here for. Nature would listen, and would provide a mirror, or maybe an echo – some responsive vision of myself that I could learn from.

As I wandered down a hill and across a meadow into the woods, a feeling of peace spread through me. It was the peace that comes with getting away from a tense situation and feeling freedom to relax. A thin blanket of leaves spread across the floor of the woods, and I kicked carelessly at them as I started sifting things in my mind.

The thing that really bothered me was that all the blockades to my success came, really, from my husband, the one person I believed should be most supportive of my deepest goals. Yes, he made a lot of sense when he gave reasons for things, but the more I reflected on my marriage over the years, the more I saw that my life was actually shaped and directed by all of his notions about how things had to be, and never by what I intuitively believed should happen. So any time I spoke of my own ambitions, he would have reasons to go in a different way, and of course what could I do but bow to his lead?

Well ... what indeed? Did I really have to bow to his lead and never fulfill my purpose? That was a question I had to answer while here at Avalon. And I had been toying with one of the painful answers that could arise from the question. Did I really need to stay with my husband at all? If I knew one thing, it was that my path was certainly not the path of organized religion, and it was organized religion that had hounded people so badly about sticking with dead-end marriages. But, was I in a dead-end marriage? I didn't think that was a given. But it was the question at hand, because if one partner is simply hung out to dry for decades on end, how can that really be called a marriage?

I kicked at a small stone on the path in front of me and it danced off into the leaves. The sun broke through the trees periodically, but I was mostly in the shade and liked it that way. It left the bite of the morning to really wake me and refresh me. It kept my thoughts clear. And with that clarity, I began tackling the whole topic of my marriage from a different angle than I was used to doing.

Here I was in a program that was supposed to address addictions, of which I had none. But I knew there was a value at Avalon for certain people, just as there's valuable psychological work. The idea is to go back to the beginning, to see *why* people believe the things they believe and do the things they do. This I knew from my own interest in self-improvement, and through my work as a career counselor. But did that method apply in a case where the issues weren't about me, but about how my husband chose to direct my life? I doubted it. In that case, we probably had to go into *his* past and see why he felt such a need to control.

Going into my husband's past would be easier anyway, because thinking of my own past was too hurtful. A lot of crummy memories of a mom who dominated and a dad who did nothing to get involved, a hailstorm I caused that destroyed our crops, a swing that ran me into rosebush thorns for my own protection, never playing with kids who might be a good influence, and having instead to play with cousins who abused me.

Yeah, they were crummy memories, because it makes you sick to think of what kids have to go through growing up, makes you wonder how half of us turn out normal at all. But in the end, as I trudged deeper into the woods and hoped I was getting too far away to make it to the first session on time, I couldn't help but feel some curiosity. If I panned through my memories with a specific goal, would I find what I was looking for? Was it possible to find clues about my own direction so many years later as I neared the golden age of fifty? And tougher still, would it be possible to find some sort of key to get around the tyranny of a restrictive marriage? After all, I'd dealt with a tyrannical mother all my life. It made sense that I might just find a technique or two.

As the questions swirled, I couldn't help myself, and my focus began to shift from the canopy of trees I was walking under to my life long ago, to fragmented stories I had from before I was born. Those set the stage for my own early years. As my focus shifted, my stomach tightened. It was hard to go back to those memories of home.

Chapter Four

If you want to talk pioneers, you might as well talk about my grandparents and their family, my dad and crew. Of course I don't mean American pioneers of the 18th and 19th centuries, but Canadian pioneers of the 20th. And heck, I'm not going to sit here and list out my whole family tree. I'll spare you that. But if there's any way to quite understand my parents, and I'm not entirely sure there is, it has got to be through knowing why they saw life the way they did. After all, we've got that good old adage about walking a mile in someone else's moccasins, even if most of us don't follow that advice. If I've learned one thing about getting beyond your past, it's that you've got to try seeing why someone treated you the way they did.

When you consider that my grandparents were forced out of their village in Russia during the revolution, and upon their return, were given ten acres to divide among six children (as well as their families), and that so little land could never support their farming needs, it's no big wonder that they took a chance at homesteading in Canada, where land was being handed to those who would develop it. The year was 1929, my dad was 14, and after a trek to Quebec City and then on to northern Alberta, the family faced the land they could call their own.

Trees.

That's what their land was. Trees. My grandmother took one look and, like the stoic woman she had to be, uttered not a sound. Tears streamed down her face. They had given up very little in exchange for absolutely nothing. Or, nothing solid. There was land here, and there was potential. But all they could do with it was go to work.

In a day, they had a shelter of sod and branches, and that is where they slept, not just that night, but for many nights, weathering thunderstorms and mosquitoes during the five weeks it took them to build a more permanent home – a 16'x20' log cabin. Everything was built by hand. Everything was cooked over an open fire. Now you tell me this doesn't start to explain a unique worldview.

Leaving ten acres in Russia didn't raise much of state for the family, and as winter started to settle in, the little money was petering out. They didn't know what to expect of an Alberta winter. They had no notion they could face temperatures of 40 and 50 degrees below zero for days at a time. They were shocked into the harshest facts of their new reality when their cache of potatoes froze inside their house and went to waste.

I admit that I find it melodramatic when parents start in with the old "When I was your age" bit. Walking miles to school through many feet of snow is the stereotypical martyr's speech, isn't it? But that's exactly what happened. Dad and two of his younger brothers walked about three miles to school every day through Alberta's unkind winters and on into spring. And you'll love this: the school was taught in English. Think they knew a lick of English?

They learned, of course. Couldn't accomplish much without understanding the language, and need was a pretty good push for them. My dad made it through a whopping two years of school, achieving third grade before having to quit school to work on the farm. After all, by then he was sixteen. No more of this education nonsense.

Don't ask me how, because I don't know, and I might not want to bore you with the details if I did, but somehow they managed, even though they couldn't harvest their first crop for two years. The entire land had to be cleared before they could farm it. They got along somehow and that lets us zip on forward about ten years. My dad was twenty seven and could finally afford his own parcel of land. He moved out from his parents' home and into a two-room house he built himself.

You can see why I'd grant my father an individualized view of the world – because *his* world *was* extreme, and was born of necessities at the bottom of Maslow's famous pyramid of needs – food, shelter, warmth. Education and self-actualization weren't on his chart, he didn't have charts, or books. He was struggling with the basics.

My mom's family, shoot, they had it easy. By the time they immigrated to Canada in 1939, the place was practically metropolitan. Land was cleared, homes were built. You could actually move into a house on cultivated land without lifting a finger. Talk about convenience! Of course that left you with the continued farming of the place, but what's that when it's all set to go? Ok, farming isn't my picture of the easy life, but I can't shake the images of what my dad must have gone through.

Also without a formal education, my mom had the chance to go to school on her arrival and match my dad's educational level by achieving 3rd grade. By then, she was fourteen, and that was plenty of education for a woman. So she began working as a maid and nanny for a wealthy family.

Around then, she met my father. Around then, my father was buying his own land. You do the math. The two-room home my father built was for his bride-to-be, my mother, 16 when they married. He was twenty seven. Unusual for almost anyone's standards these days. But remember, it was a different world. And no wonder their views were so different than my own.

There was one matter that stood out most of all. One matter that would make the biggest difference in their point of view and would so profoundly impact me that it could be argued as the defining period of my life, even though it was my parents' issue, and even though it happened some time before I was born. That matter was my brother, Alexander.

Chapter Five

My mother was seventeen when Alexander was born. A different world? Maybe. But just like now, seventeen is a little on the young side for giving birth. It was the fact my mom was sure made the difference in Alexander's health – a child who was born underweight and sickly. He had colic and dysentery at the same time. He had rectal bleeding. And she – my mother – got blamed.

The women of the community came to help. They offered a great deal of support. And they offered their wisdom. Or, that's what it was supposed to be. But that brand of wisdom included making one point clear: she was young, she was weak, and she could not be a good mother. Had she been stronger, the baby would be strong. It was, in fact, her weakness that brought such an unhealthy babe.

One local woman concocted an herbal remedy. The boy was later taken to the hospital some 30 miles away. Everything was done that could be done. Alexander took his last breath on December 18 of the year he was born as the women stood about the crib. He was two months and twelve days old.

That last breath spelled a certain doom for me. I was not conceived yet. I had no say in anything about it. But that last breath was momentous for my parents, more so than for some. Why? Because my parents believed that it was my mother's fault, her age, her weakness, that led to the child's death. And with that belief, how could they not then adopt a parenting style of strength? Of brutal strength?

My father cried for days about the baby. My mother was miserable with guilt. The funeral took place on December 29 and there was no autopsy, no clue about the baby's real cause of death. None needed. Everyone knew the reason. No point to make it linger.

As it does for everyone, life meandered on. No matter how much the baby might linger in their thoughts, life still meant farming and getting by. And end of the next summer, my father was inducted into the Canadian Army. It was August of 1943. My mother was 18, alone, without electricity, running water, or telephone through yet another Alberta winter. Neighbors checked in with her, but if you take even a moment to think about what a winter like that would feel like, it's no wonder that my mother decided to follow my father to his second training camp, just to be near him and to get a job. She worked in a tomato canning factory.

Meanwhile, Dad was an expert marksman, winning all sorts of trophies for accuracy. The excitement of all this acted as a slow-motion eraser to memories of a lost child. When my father was finally discharged from the army in April, 1946, he returned to the farm with my mom. She was already pregnant, and I was born two months later on June 3. Mom was twenty one now, a better age for giving birth, perhaps, but she was deathly nervous. When handed her baby for nursing, she found that the milk wouldn't come. She would starve this baby. She could see that right away. This baby was going to die, and she would be blamed again. She knew she couldn't handle that guilt. What would she do?

The hospital staff was there to calm her and work with her, and after a few days, the milk finally arrived. After ten days in the hospital, we made it to the two-room log cabin. Home. As a family. And this baby wouldn't die on them.

But how could they know that? As far as they could see, the life and death of a child might as well be a coin toss. If they could do anything to affect that toss, they would. They would grab on tight, make sure death had little or no chance to get to their little one, and never give up that grip. That was their strategy. And I was lucky enough to get every little bit of that kind of love.

Chapter Six

I remember my mother's eyes, staring at me, all glassy like the window they were looking through. It was a cold stare, an all-seeing stare. "Careful now. Don't swing too high," said the eyes. And I just blinked and turned my face away, drifting back into a quiet reverie. There *was* no swinging high on the swing my dad built. It was for sitting, because if you tried to get it moving, you would hit a rose bush on every back-swing.

It wasn't built there as deliberate torture. No, my parents were never so cruel. But here, from an overhang outside the kitchen window, my mother could watch. Everything was done by hand in our home, and that meant she passed most of her hours in the one area that acted as living room, dining room, and kitchen. Food preparation kept her close by that window, which kept her in control. She would not lose her baby to a swinging accident, that was certain. So she stared, and watched, and made sure death was not lurking. "Not too high," she seemed to say. And what could I do but obey? I wasn't about to swing into the rose bush.

From an early age, I felt the presence of my brother, Alexander – not as a friend, nor as a fiend, but a shadow around my mother. I didn't think of it as Alexander, of course. In fact, I didn't think of it much at all. Too young for any of that. But there was always this childhood curiosity as I wondered, "Is this it? Am I to sit here and never move? Is that what it is to be a child? And then, when I am grown, I will find myself working in a tiny room all my life until I am dead?"

I would look back to my mother, still staring through the window, and she seemed to nod "Yes" in answer to my questions. Probably she was nodding, pleased that I sat so still on the swing. But to me, she was saying, "Yes, my dear. That is all. You are to sit there and be safe, and all will be well." And of course she was right – she was my mother.

In retrospect, it's easy to ask: why wouldn't she see it like that? For my mom, life had been pretty consistent. Life was hard, yet always the same, in the old country. Then they moved to Canada, set up a home here, and lived the same way. She married my father, moved into his small, two-room cabin, and continued again in the very same way. Step back from it all and look at the general stroke of her life, she could only have seen a woman's role in a very narrow way. She could only see that life was a struggle for survival and she would be convinced that a child was a fragile thing. Had to be. She had already lost half of her own.

In an age of TVs and computers, and everything you can think of to entertain you in the local malls and bowling allies and movie theatres and so much more, it's easy to picture the other reason why Mom had to watch me while doing her chores. There wasn't a damned other thing to watch. The house we lived in for my first few years was not so unlike my mom's or dad's houses when they lived with their parents in Canada. It was the home my dad built along with help from his brothers – all of 200 square feet, two rooms, one for living, one for sleeping. You can believe me when I say our little family was in a cozy package together.

Cozy? It was small, rather than warm. It was made of logs, and had a stove to keep the place toasty. If my mom wasn't cleaning the place, she was over that stove. After all, she was from Russia, so that's where a wife belonged. The kitchen was her pride. It's the role she knew for a woman and the role I learned from her.

While I sat in silent contemplation on a swing that I didn't dare move, and Mom peeled skins from potatoes and watched me, Dad managed 160 acres of farmland. That was no small feat for a one-man operation. Outside we had a chicken coop, pig sty, horse and cow barn, a granary, a shed for farm equipment and an ice house. One part of the land dipped down toward the creek. Most everything was farmed. Dad worked it hard enough to turn a profit over time, which meant all the daylight hours he was alone on the land. Just the way it should be, the role he knew.

O

Ok, so it's not much of a challenge to start seeing things through my parents' eyes. Different life, different beliefs, etc. But it gets a whole lot more complicated if one looks at archetypes, because like it or not, we all play some sort of role.

No need to start debating free will, I'm not going to deny it. And if you get the idea of archetypes, you understand that playing an archetypal role doesn't have anything to do with pre-destination. It refers to tendencies any one of us might have. And there's nothing hokey about the concept either. We all have natural survival and defense mechanisms. If you buy that idea, then 1+1= archetypes. Why? Because when someone plays a role in a family, it is more about survival than anything else.

The firstborn has no one to compete with for love from the parents, the second one does, and there are a million studies that show how much love, touch and affection from parents impacts a baby's well-being. The third child is joining a crowded family. By the time the fourth comes around, the older kids are in school and the parents have time to give more affection. And so on. All children need love and attention, and birth position has a lot to do with how much they get and how they perceive themselves within a family. No wizardry here.

If we really want to shed light on any family, understanding the four basic archetypes of children can take us a long way. My mom and dad played their parts beautifully, and so did I, but not quite as you might imagine.

Mom was the firstborn of her family, and that made her the family "hero," so to speak. There are positive and negative aspects surrounding each archetype, and we'd be suspicious if there weren't. There isn't a personality on the planet that's all bad or all good. From an early age, Mom had high expectations placed on her. She was meant to set an example, to be responsible, to live up to her parents' ideals of the perfect child. And like so many born in that slot, she worked hard to live up to these expectations. This is how she would find her love. She became a perfectionist in the things she did, taking on her parents' conservative viewpoints not only to please them, but also to avoid conflict in general. Organization was key. Image was key. Blame came fast on those who bucked the system or did not follow expectation. She did what was expected of her. It was what kept the world together and, so far as she knew, what allowed one to find love.

Meanwhile, my dad was third born in his family – the "lost child." This is a tough slot to fall into – not because of the person a third child becomes, but because it's a natural position for feeling left out. Any parent will tell you, hands are full with two kids, one to each adult. Add a third, you're just begging for headaches. That's the scene a third kid comes into, and the child often feels it. "Dad's already got a kid. Mom's already got a kid. That leaves me on my own." So the third child tends to feel lonely, or to isolate. The kid is private, generally apprehensive, and tends to stay out of people's ways. Like so many others, my dad was raised with the understanding that a man goes out, does hard work and provides for his family. The woman cooks, cleans and raises the kids. That had to have been his preference anyway, simply by virtue of being third in line. While amazed that Dad could tend to such a large farm on his own, I also know he enjoyed the work, hours and hours on his own, tending to what he could do so well, and quietly succeeding over the years. It suited him well.

And it suited my mom well. It left her in charge of me. This gave her molding time, which she desperately wanted to ensure my safety and happiness. I would fit her expectations and society's expectations. I would look good. I would be obedient. I would share her views, and on and on. I would be her firstborn child, her hero, her greatest achievement.

Only, she'd already had a firstborn. And that lingering shadow meant I could never fill her expectations.

Chapter Seven

Alexander did hover. He was absolutely real in my mother's mind. Never once did she utter his name, but so often in her disappointments of me, I could practically see her envisioning what a good child would do, what her good child would do. Of course I could never imagine it in that way as a child, but as the years progressed, so did my understanding. There was never a right answer for my mother. There was no satisfying her, because she was in love with an idea – and that idea was an ideal.

Alexander was not truly my mother's first child. She had no time to know him. The idea of Alexander, that was her child. The idea believed as my mother did; looked as my mother wished it to; acted as my mother wished it to; impressed other people as my mother wished it to. *Why can't you be more like your brother?* was the unspoken reference point by which I was measured.

Of course it was all in my mother's mind and, as far as I know, was possibly ever-changing. I could be never like my brother, though the good Lord knows I tried to be. And when trying my best didn't work, and then trying my best again didn't work, and then trying my best again didn't work, I was backed into a corner that would breed me for leading a gang, torturing animals, and turning our small town into havoc. In the old heredity vs. environment banter, score one for environment.

But there's a lot of story adding up to that. Part of that story had to do with a swing that I couldn't swing on. The swing was built so I could be watched and slowly learn that I was to be monitored and cared for without fail. No wing-stretching. If I would one day fly, it would be because my mother had lifted me into the air, and not because I had jumped.

From the earliest days, I was within a few feet of my mother most the time. That could hardly be helped, since our living area was 10 by 15 feet and nearly everything about our lives was done there. Mom had one of those old washboards, discolored across a few of the ridges, that she ran down into a huge tub filled with soap and water. Beside it she would stand with our dresses and stockings and the filthy clothes from my father. She'd lean in and throttle the clothes across the thing methodically, robotically. The kitchen had an old metal pan that was used for a sink. It had no plumbing. She would fill it with water from the boiler, which was attached to the wood stove. She had to pick the pan up, lug it outdoors, and fling the water into the yard just to empty it. Rain or shine, summer or winter, that was the way of the pan. And my mom would stand at that pan preparing meals or, after we ate, she'd be there wiping dried beans and potatoes off our plates. From fetching the water to bringing the empty pan back indoors, washing clothes, preparing food and doing dishes in our home was tedious and tiresome.

I would watch. I would ask questions. How you cooked was how you were judged. How you kept the home spoke volumes about you, and I was determined that one day I would be a perfect wife like my mother was. I would know how to cook, sew, milk cows and feed the chickens. These were what made a woman valuable. At least on that point I was clear. I would some day be valuable to a good man if I watched enough, if I asked enough.

I was careful, though. Oh yes, I was careful because I knew. I had asked once to peel the potatoes for dinner and Mom beamed on me with pleasure. "You know how then?" she asked. I nodded and she handed me a knife and 'tater. I wasn't a dozen strokes into the task when she wrested them both from me. She wasn't beaming any more. "All this time I've shown you and you're going to butcher our potatoes like that? We don't have potatoes to spare, you know."

And I'd once asked to run my stockings on the washboard and hang them myself, but I caught them along the side of the board and tore them. Mom's grimace was a thing to see as she swatted my hand and stole back the stockings from me. "Never create more work when doing work," she told me. "What will a man think of something like that?" So I was careful because I knew. I must ask questions, but I must never get involved. That was the way of learning and one day as a valuable wife, I would get it all right.

When I wasn't indoors watching my mother, or playing with a hand-made toy (store-bought were out of the question), I was out on the can't-swing swing, or playing outdoors, in sight of a living room window. During the summer, I often helped Mom with the flower garden surrounding the house – another job that made a woman worth her salt. Of course helping consisted mostly of watching Mother line bottles carefully, upside-down, to border the garden, and then as she lined the flowers just as carefully, organizing them so that their colors were neatly arranged. "No sense having flowers just run off wild," she would tell me. And I would nod, understanding that running wild was a thing to be avoided. I would stand close by, seeing how she dug each seed hole just so and covered it just so in case I was ever asked to lend a hand in the dirt. I was not. And of course I knew better than to broach the subject.

I would find myself beside the garden again as the cold weather set in and frost had stunned the flowers and put their colors to shame. There was no mourning them, no letting their barren stems stand frigid without petals. The moment cold came for them, Mother was into the dirt with a hoe, razing the lot of them. She erased them in minutes and if their lives would ever have meaning again, it was in the flowers that would bloom the next year.

There's no question – Mom's rigid perfectionism and hard work helped provide for us. We had almost nothing at home that wasn't provided for directly on our farm. Dad milled some of the grain he grew for our flour. Mom not only tended her little army of flowers, but also substantial gardens full of vegetables. In the fall she would jar much of what was left from the garden, as well as turning berries from bushes all around our property into jam. All our family meat came from slaughtered animals. Milk, cheese and eggs came from the cows and chickens. In short, they needed only a few staples from town – sugar, salt, baking powder, and the like. Dad would make a weekly trek into town for the staples and the mail.

Of course it wasn't like hopping into the car and bolting on down to the store. Town was five miles away and we had no car. Every week, Dad would hitch up Dolly and Jessie to a wagon and drive on in. I'll never forget those two horses. They were big, black, and mean, even if you'd never guess it by their names. As a child, I was terrified of them because they would look at me with their huge brown eyes, and if I got close, they'd snort and stomp their feet. Then they'd snort some more because of the dust they kicked up. They probably weren't much different than any horses in the world. I mean, every horse has its personality, and there are plenty of ornery ones. I doubt if Dolly and Jessie were worse than any other horses, but as a kid, anything so huge, stolid, and leering was a thing to be feared.

Once in town, Dad would sell off his quota of grain, farmers were only allowed to sell so much at a time, which would cover the purchases he needed to make and a little extra that would go into savings. We survived from week to week and if things didn't go smoothly during the farm season, it meant that Dad would have to take on winter work off the farm to make things work.

I seldom got to visit town with my father. It was a substantial trip, eating up half the day, and Dad didn't need someone slowing things down. So I would remain home within a few feet of my mother and we would pass the day as usual, watching for his safe return. During one of these trips, though, we were convinced that Dad wouldn't return safely at all. It was on that day that I learned why Mother was so impatient with my shortcomings, why she seldom let me put my hand to things. God was angry with me, and he said so out loud. And if God was angry with me, it only made sense that my mother would be too.

Chapter Eight

Dad had hitched up Dolly and Jessie, checked that the reins and harness were all strapped on correctly, looked up to the grey sky one last time, then stepped up onto the wagon. Mom and I stood in front of the house as we often did to see him off. He nodded curtly at us before flicking the reins and moving the wagon.

He'd been gone maybe half an hour when it started to rain and Mom and I moved from the garden into the house. Mom tidied up for a few minute while the rain turned steady and seemed to be settling in for a long day of tireless soaking. I watched it through a window and saw little streams forming in the dirt paths around the house. Then came the downpour.

People today know what rain sounds like on a shingled roof. It is a sound many of us are in love with, it makes for the best nights of falling asleep or the best mornings of sleeping in, if we are so lucky as to have the opportunity. But the sound of rain on shingles is very different from the sound of rain on a wooden roof which seems to absorb the impact and sound, perhaps only because it is thicker than shingles over plywood. When the rain poured down in buckets on that solid wooden house of ours, the sound was awesome and glorious. As I stood at the window that day, I closed my eyes and listened to the music of the pelting rain.

Then the ground shook with thunder, and that was music to my ears as well. Thunder. Was there anything quite so powerful? The sky lit up a few times each minute and the thunder clapped behind the light. And my little four-year-old brain got to working. What was it that could make such a sound? So I asked. "Mamma, where does thunder come from?"

When I turned around, I saw that my mom was standing nervously by the window that looked out on our front pathway, out to where my dad had stepped into the wagon not long ago. Mom looked sideways at me. "Same place everything comes from," she said flatly, something different in her voice. "God makes the thunder. He makes it when He's angry and stomps His feet about in heaven." She turned back to the window and kept staring.

God was angry? That was a scary thought. If He had made everything, having an angry God had to be a dangerous situation. It made me wonder, and I asked out loud: "Why is God angry? What makes Him angry?"

Mom let out a loud sigh through her nose. She didn't turn to me this time. "He gets angry because people are bad. When people do bad things, God stomps His feet in heaven."

She went silent again and I got to thinking. There weren't too many people around where we lived. Even in town there were only a handful of families and shops. So if God was angry with someone around here, chances were good that I'd done something to upset Him. I must have been bad. But what could I have done to create such a thunderstorm as this? I couldn't fathom a thing, but God was often a critical part of Mom's answers about things, so she must have known Him pretty well. If He was angry, I knew it was with me. I had to figure out what I had done that was wrong and make sure I didn't pull that again.

Suddenly, the thrilling sound of a downpour on the roof turned to the startling sound of something more, as if our roof were collapsing around us. I looked quickly to the window and saw massive chunks of hail clattering to the ground, crashing and bouncing in sudden heaps across our pathways, out in the garden, and as far as I could see through the sheets of falling white. And then I heard it: a sound I'd never met and a sound I hoped I'd never meet again. My mother, sturdy, solid, controlled, began to whimper out loud. As I looked her way, I saw her lose her strength and sink slowly to her knees beside the window as her body shook.

My eyebrows furled and my eyes squinted just a bit. Was it real? Was I seeing what I thought I was seeing? I crept towards her with my hand held out and as I reached her, I touched her shoulder and asked, "What is it Mamma? Why are you crying?"

Mom sniffled and took a few gasping breaths. "Your father," she managed to say. "If he is caught in this …."

She didn't continue, and she didn't need to. I understood exactly what it meant to be caught under a storm of hail like this. But there was something worse than the notion of my father in the storm. There was the notion of why the storm had hit us at all. Was God that angry with me?

Mother rose suddenly to her feet and rummaged in through the kitchen things. She pulled out a cast iron frying pan and walked quickly to the door. Carefully, she opened the door just enough for sliding the pan through and she held it out to catch some of the hail. Within seconds, the hail stopped falling and my mother brought the pan back indoors. "You have to try to catch the hail," she told me. "You have to use a cast iron pan. Then it will stop." It was incredible to think you could stop God from being so angry with just a cast iron pan, but the proof was in a cast iron frying pan full of hail. Mom had somehow managed to stop the storm. I would remember always. *Stop hail with a frying pan.*

Mom sat down wearily in a chair. We both knew that Dad would still be on his way to town when the hail struck. It would only take one or two hailstones that size to knock him out, and the rest would finish the job. Neither of us cried, but Mom wrapped her arms around me and we sat there quietly, wondering what we would do.

○

It was some hours later when Dad pulled up our dirt driving path with Dolly and Jessie. The storm did not hit so widely as we thought. Mom and I were astonished, so sure that my dad was gone for good. We ran out to meet him, but he just drove the horses slowly, surveying the slush that now buried our yard, our garden, our fields and fields of crops. When he neared us, he pulled up on the reins and got out to stand beside us, silent because he was looking.

"Everything?" asked my mother quietly.

Dad nodded. "Yes. It's all gone."

I wasn't more than four years old, but the tone in their voices told me they were desperate. And so was I, because I had an inkling. "Daddy?" He looked sadly into my eyes. "Where does hail come from?"

He breathed deeply. "When God gets really angry with people," he told me, "He throws hail down from heaven."

So I was right. I didn't just cause the thunder, I caused the hail too. And because of that hail, we had lost nearly everything – our garden and all our crops. I knew we depended on those crops to buy food in town. I knew we depended on them for our flour. I knew we depended on the garden for all our vegetables and for everything my mom would preserve for winter use. It was all gone because I had done something bad. I had –

That was it. I knew. I suddenly knew, and the tears began to stream down my face. I had stolen a cookie from the cookie jar. And my parents were being punished for what I had done. I would never have thought that God could be so angry for such a little thing, but the thunder and the hail said it all. I looked out now across the fields and fields that I had destroyed.

Chapter Nine

We've all been horrified when reading the newspapers. Amidst all the good in people, and I mean most of us even if we've each got our issues, there are some people who make us cringe and turn ill. Many of these are people who have somehow lost their reason and have slipped into evil to the point that they commit gruesome crime against humanity. Others are people who have taken delight in evil and have made it their life and their habit.

Maybe we can't always know what drove a person into some action, and we don't know if they slipped, or if this is who they are. Among these gruesome deeds, there is perhaps nothing so vile as a crime against a child, a child who is innocent and defenseless.

My dad was so "hands off" that my life was left to my mother's will. And the simple fact is that she was never one of these people we read about in the papers. She didn't physically torture me. She didn't murder me. And knowing her history, it is not so surprising that she raised me the way she did.

So where is the problem? The problem is that my mother was not so unique, and that there are many parents who raise their kids in a similar way – protective to the point of strangulation, manipulative to the point of unreal world views, controlling to the point that the child develops no sense of self.

Kids are told about Santa Claus, and while old Santa is as real as real gets, he is real in the sense that he is the spirit of giving. There are tales kids grow up with, only to shake off the story and find the truth it represents. So the whole thing about God stomping His feet in heaven to make thunder wouldn't have been that big an issue, except in my house, that was the way of the world. Many years later in school, I challenged my science teacher on the topic of thunder and was humiliated in front of the class. There were no scientific explanations of the world in my family.

On issues of sex or just about anything else, I was told stories to encourage a world view very much like my mother's. God is vengeful to those who step out of line, and out of line meant out of tradition. A woman's place is in the kitchen. The "honor your father and mother" bit was used to prove that Mother was always right. Believing that there is a God who wishes for order is one thing, acknowledging that many women are wonderfully fulfilled by taking care of home and children is easy enough, and remembering that parents *are* often right when their children think otherwise – that's important too.

But there is a balance for each of these things. If tradition was always God's will, then we might still be sacrificing animals or even humans in the name of our god. If women had always followed the housemother role, how many of the world's most influential people would disappear from our history books? If Mother was always right, we would have to admit that all the abused and neglected children in the world deserved exactly what they got.

For my part, I believed these things, because I believed that Mother *was* always right. Therefore, I knew what role I should play in the world and I knew to step carefully lest I disturb God's fair mood. And what resulted really was a need to look to my mom for approval. I tried to help with potatoes and had the peeler wrested away. I tried to help with mending clothes and had the needle quickly taken. I dared not approach the flowers. Even when I spoke with people, I found that my mother often monitored what I said, then swooped in for corrections, so that before long, I would look to her before I even opened my mouth. In other words, what seems like small matters built into something not small. It was the repetition of little things, like the constantly dripping water of the infamous Chinese water torture.

At the same time, the little things were not always so little in our family. There were some things my parents did that were out and out wrong. And then there were the doozies that drove me away from them, and eventually drove me to Avalon. As I continued to reflect on my past, to consider just what Jean was asking when she said, "Tell me about yourself," my mind swept across so many of my childhood experiences. The little things added up into something big and I felt that so many of the definitely ill choices my parents made were the doozies that were buried deep inside me.

Chapter Ten

The little things continued over the years, my mom showing that decisions were not for the young. Mom was there to protect and direct at all times, and that did not just mean pointing the way. It meant *being* the way. This was manifested in so many ways, and among them, how I dressed. And in particular, how I dressed for one event.

There were times when Dad didn't travel alone to town. I don't know if Mom just needed to see other faces or if she was itching to see the kinds of things other people would actually buy. On the rarest occasion, she'd splurge and pick up some lipstick when she was low, but that was about it.

So from time to time, we all piled onto the horse wagon and made our way those five miles into town. These were the best of times for me — scenery, sure; buildings, yeah; and people. Especially people. It was almost hard to remember that there were people besides Mom and Dad and the family living across the creek from us.

Beckermans was the only general store in town. Besides Beckermans, there was the post office, a blacksmith shop and a grain elevator. A hamlet of fewer than 25 people really couldn't support much else. The general store carried all the staples my dad went to town for, and the other knick knacks people might want — toiletries, perfume, shoes, clothes, tools, you name it.

When you pulled up to Beckermans, you'd see one of those old gas tanks outside, the kind with gas inside the glass container up top. You had to hand crank the thing to fill your car. It was always a little dark inside the store because they didn't have any wired electricity, just a generator in the far corner to run a few dim lights. There were oiled, wooden floors, shelves everywhere, and a payphone near the front. Through a door in the back were the living quarters. My dad seemed to like Mr. Beckerman. They shook hands the way men should, with a smile, looking eye to eye.

I didn't know what they spoke of in the store because they spoke in English and we only spoke Ukrainian at home. That was still the native tongue for both my parents, and it was the only thing I was exposed to. So while they batted away tongues, I would stand in awe of the rows and rows of canned goods and the barrels of dry goods scattered through the store.

I remember the first time I saw a wheel of cheese there and I called my dad's attention away from Mr. Beckerman. "What is it?" I asked him.

Dad took the can that Mr. Beckerman was handing him, then looked my way. "It's cheese," he said.

I gave Dad a doubtful look. "That's not cheese. Mom makes cheese at home and it doesn't look anything like this."

Dad smiled. "It's still cheese," he assured me. He turned back to Mr. Beckerman, said some things in English, and the two of them laughed together while the clerk looked at me, amused. I smiled politely, then turned away, hoping they weren't laughing at me.

I saw that my mom was walking toward the back door that lead into the store owner's quarters. She always did this when we went into town. Normally I would spend my time looking in through a glass showcase in the store, where they kept lipsticks and dolls and beautiful ornaments – things I knew I could never have, but things I dreamed of owning. That glass showcase was magic for me. It represented a different kind of life, a kind of life that others had. It was my secret dream to have that kind of life and that showcase was part of the dream.

But on this trip when I learned that cheese could look different if it wanted to, I watched curiously through the showcase as Mom knocked on the door to the Beckerman home and Mrs. Beckerman opened up. They exchanged a few whispered words, and she handed Mom a box. Mom's face turned bright red as she took the thing, turned, and tried to make her way outdoors unnoticed. She hurried toward our wagon to shove the box under the seat. But I had followed, and when she turned, I was standing on the porch with my head cocked to one side. "What's in the box, Mom?" I asked her.

Poor Mom. Her face had nearly lost its initial flush when she saw me there. She was beet red again in a second. "Nothing for you to think about. I'll tell you when you're older."

I wanted to be older right away. Growing up had so many obvious advantages, and this was just one more to add to the list. Another was make-up, something I wasn't allowed to explore for many more years, yet something my mom took very seriously for herself.

Her impact on other people was important to my mother. And no kidding about it, I loved watching her get ready for trips into town. She would curl her hair with bobby pins and then style it when it dried. She would form waves of hair, beginning at the part and working across her head. Then she'd use an eyebrow pencil to enlarge her beauty mark before adding a hint of blush to her cheeks. And finally, she'd top it off with dark red lipstick to match a deep magenta, taffeta dress. Boy, my mother knew how to do it. I was too young to notice, but I'll bet she had all sorts of men looking her way when she was all done up like that.

I was all of five years old. No need to tell you that Mom wouldn't let me touch the make-up, and I wouldn't be allowed to till I was sixteen. "Too much flair," she'd tell me. "Not good for a girl until she's ready to get married." Presumably, that meant at around age sixteen.

At least when I was five, I'm sure my mom was right, make-up probably wasn't a good idea. Anyway, she could hardly afford lipstick for herself. But a *dress!* If only I could wear one dress that wasn't Mom-made. A dress from a real store – the kind that fit the glass showcase dream of owning something truly beautiful. I wouldn't care about make-up or growing older just yet. If I had one store-bought dress for wearing to town, to look as beautiful as the girls there – I would be in child heaven!

The tragedy, if I can call it that, the five-year-old mind holds a different measure of the awesome and the awful, is that Mom had a two-part agenda that conflicted with itself. On the one hand, she was all about making ends meet, which is one of those old-fashioned values we could probably do with more of these days. On the other hand, she was set on making sure we looked good for other people. The first of these meant that all of my clothes were homemade, which conflicted with the second because I didn't think Mom had a sense of style or design for how she dressed me.

Out on the farm, that wasn't much of an issue. The horses weren't going to say anything, even though they stared me down with those mean old eyes. The chickens clucked at everything, so I didn't take any special offense when they clucked about my clothing. But when we went to town, I hated looking frumpy. Worse yet, I would be going to school before long, I knew that; my mother knew that. The question was, could she bear for me to look homemade when image was so important to her?

Eventually, the day arrived when Mom didn't have much choice. We were invited to a wedding, and my mother hadn't the time to make a dress to make the right impression. So finally – *finally!* – we went to the big town, the town that had the hospital I was born in, where they had shops galore. I went with a dress in mind. One of the small specialty shops was a clothing store for children called Bo Peep. If I had dreams about how beautiful it would be inside, the dreams fell short. It was a small store, painted white on the outside and yellow inside – not a light, cold yellow, but more of a warm, inviting, and golden hue. As we walked in, I could hardly fathom that so many clothes existed in the world, much less in our little part of it. And the dresses – oh, they were far more beautiful than the images I had dared to conjure. The experience felt luxurious. I breathed in the moment and began sifting through the dresses. They felt good in my hands. The sewing was perfect; the styles set my little mouth a-gaping. My mother was my hero for bringing me here!

As much as I loved nearly all the dresses I saw, two stood out. I was almost ready to call my mother over and have her pick between them, when, before my eyes: a dark blue velvet dress cut perfectly, lace around the neck and cuffs. It was my dress. I knew it. The other two didn't matter any more, and I turned to call my mom.

But, as I turned, she was right in front of me.

With a dress in hand.

With a dress possibly more ugly than any she had ever made. The thing was a travesty to behold, and insult to the very notion of little girls. Who – *who!* – would design such a thing and sell it? Did they *mean* to ruin an innocent kid's childhood?

Worse yet, what was my mom doing *carrying* the thing? But that didn't take long to solve. A smile spread across her face which might as well have been Cruella's smile in that moment, as she stepped toward me, arms held out to measure the dress against me in her mind's eye. Well, there wasn't a question any more: my awful homemade dresses weren't awful anymore. Presuming she didn't intend torture, they were awful because her eye couldn't tell the difference because her taste was terrible.

In that moment, with my heart sinking fast and the up-coming wedding flashing across my imagination, I started to protest my mom's selection. But as her smile fell, she stunned me with a look that seemed to ask, "Excuse me? Are you doing what I think you're doing? Are you actually challenging me when I'm going so far as to buy you a dress?" My own eyes went wide like those of a startled horse. I forced a smile, took the dress in hand, and held it up before myself in a mirror. There it was, in all its ridiculous glory – white, see-through nylon with a white under slip and covered in red velvet cherries. It had a sash for a belt, red cotton on one side, pink-and-white checked on the other. It couldn't have been in fashion in any era I know of. The thing was gaudy and at five years old, I knew it. I swallowed my pride and my voice. I looked at my mom and forced one more smile. So this was what buying dresses with Mother was like. I would remember in the future not to protest her choice. I would also remember that it was pointless to desire a dress from the store.

Chapter Eleven

So for my first many seasons, I knew only life beside my mother – within just feet of her at all times. I generally did not see others unless they were family or, on the rarest occasion, store clerks. The kids I saw in town were kids I saw from a distance. I knew there was a girl about my age living just down the road, but I wasn't allowed to play with her. See, things ran in a pretty funny way. There were three groups of adults in and around the small community: the Ukrainian Catholics, which this girl and her family were part of; the Ukrainian non-Catholics, which included my family; and English-speaking people. These distinctions were literal barriers around whom you did and did not hang out with. So while there was a girl living on the farm next door, I never got to play with her, which meant that playtime with any other kid amounted to playtime with cousins. One of them was a boy a couple years older than I who joined his siblings in the thrill of harassing me.

I don't use the word lightly. Most kids look forward to playtime. I didn't mind it in our home, where I'd get to play with some home made toy; or I'd get to perch on the sitting swing, or I'd maybe wander the fenced yard out back, dwelling in some make-believe world. But if I knew playtime was going to be at my cousins' home, I'd slip into a panic.

If my mom was set on a visit, there wasn't any telling her *no*. There wasn't any pretending I suddenly felt ill, because she figured that one out after I pulled it once or twice. The grim reality for me at age five was that I didn't have much voice about where we would go, and I was certain to suffer when playtime was spent with my cousins.

The irony was that playing with my cousins was the only time I got to spend without my mother, and that it was the one time I wanted to be closer to Mom than ever. Sunday would be a visiting day, and the three of us would trek to my aunt and uncle's house. Mother would hold my hand and pull me towards the door, often oblivious that I was practically trying to walk backwards. Sometimes she'd quip, "Good heavens, Girl, pick up your feet and walk like a lady! What have I been teaching you all this time?" We lived on a farm and there weren't too many lessons about how to walk, but she seemed to think it applied.

Up to the door we'd march. Mom would give two quick knocks, and my aunt's voice would call from the kitchen, "Come in, come in!" Mom would open the door, the three of us would step inside and there they were. My cousins. Often they were clustered like a pack of jackals, or anything else unsavory. And they'd grin, or at least it felt as if they did. They knew they had fresh prey for the afternoon and they were anxious to get the game going. My father would quickly disappear into another room to visit with his brother.

"Outdoors with you now," said our mothers. "Go and get some fresh air." And those were the words I wished Mom would say any other time, were words of doom. "Go … be free!" Any time but now. Because now, my cousins would gather 'round me and we'd head outside. "Hide and seek," they'd cry. And off they'd run. They were all stronger than I was, and they knew I could never catch them. As much as that frustrated me when I was little, eventually I learned better. This would be the best part of the day. I would take my time finding them. I would pretend to chase after them to keep the game going as long as I could.

The next game, despite my efforts, was bound to come up. At some point, I would *have* to go to the bathroom. Back on the farm, if I had to go, I'd just squat down where I was. But with my cousins around, I wasn't pulling that stunt. Using the outhouse was nearly as bad. I might think I was sneaking in there, but inevitably, one of my cousins would see me and before I was finished going, I'd be locked in. One thing I need to explain here. The outhouses locked from both sides. The inside had a hook latch to prevent the door being opened from the outside, and the outside had a latch to prevent the wind from blowing the door open when not in use.

Eventually, one of them would unlock the door. "Hey everyone, she's gotta go peepee!" he laughed, phrasing it like a little child to mock me. While the rest turned to look, he ran to me, lifted my skirt, and pulled my panties down. All my cousins doubled over in laughter.

Teasing me about my crooked teeth, tackling me, pounding me – these were their afternoon thrills. If I tried to join Mom indoors, she and my aunt would kick me right back outdoors. "We're having adult talk," I'd be told. It didn't matter that I was covered in dirt, or that Mom would sometimes find bruises on me after a visit. I presume she thought it was all part of the game.

So in all my early years, that was the time I got to spend away from my mom. Yet from that very early age, I had this desire to have some time alone, or away, without having to get pummeled by my cousins. Oh, the point isn't lost on me that I was still quite young, and that a mother *should* watch a daughter closely. But we were so joined at the hip that when I did see children face-to-face in town, I honestly did not know how to interact with them. I had no social skills, I only knew how to respond to my mother and my cousins.

And the incident of buying a dress was more than a lonely misfortune. It became clear that Mom would make my choices. In fact, I hardly knew what to say if someone asked me what I wanted if Mom wasn't around. I was accustomed to her speaking for me. There is some handy psycho jargon on the topic, and there's no question about it. Take over on your child's behalf, you're just asking for later problems because they never learn how to choose for themselves. It is the great parent challenge to balance safety with freedom, security with exploration. Too far to either side, you risk the child's physical, emotional, mental, and – dare I say it? – spiritual health.

Even as a child, I felt this entanglement. I didn't really know, though, whether it was normal because I didn't have other kids or people as models. But it sure felt strange. I hardly knew when I should talk, and if I was encouraged to speak, I anticipated motherly correction. So my words became relatively few, only because they weren't needed and were not valued.

At such an early age, though, I didn't really ponder the matter deeply enough to work out plans of escape, nor had I begun to feel suffocated. That was to come. If I'd thought about it, I'd have made sure everything I did showed my mother that I was strong, capable and she wasn't going to lose me. If she could feel that in her heart, maybe – just *maybe* – Alexander would not hover so convincingly. Maybe she could let down her guard just a little, knowing that I'd be around for a long time to come. But one day, without a moment to think it through, I gave her precisely the opposite message.

It was one of those warm summer days when not only was my mom's garden blooming, but the wild flowers all around our farm were going nuts. The land was draped in brilliant colors and perfumed with subtle, flowered scents. I was in our fenced yard out back and though Mom could keep an eye on me through one window, she was prepping vegetables for a late lunch and was probably staring instead at the sitting swing. It was a rare time when she wasn't looking.

I was humming probably a little off-tune but in love with the moment because I was outside without Mom and that was a taste of freedom that I never failed to breathe in. I was skipping around the yard, probably with an invisible friend or two. Maybe we were playing tag or I was inviting them to my invisible table for tea, when I swallowed my sounds and just stopped. There, in front of me, was an enormous cat. It wasn't moving, but was watching everything I did. Its eyes stared into mine as my lip began to quiver. Shock alone kept me from crying out straight off, and maybe that was my good luck. I backed up two, three, four steps, then turned and ran – crying at last – into the house.

Wrong place. Wrong direction. Wrong person to tell. But how could I not? I was in hysterics! Mother caught me in her arms and heard me balling about a cat as large as I was. A lynx, she decided. I could have been attacked. In the few moments when she wasn't watching, I could have been killed. Life was as delicate as that. No looking back now. The rope that bound me to my mother turned to a chain and throttled me inwards once more. For my safety? Yes. Perhaps. But it was the last time for a long while that I would be allowed outside alone. It was the last time Mom would let me out of her sight.

Except for one fact she couldn't control. I was almost six. I would soon be going to school. At last, social skills in me or not, I would begin talking and playing with other kids. And there my mother would have no chance to watch, to correct, to decide who I should play with. There, I would bloom into something new.

But as I said early on, score one for environment. I would bloom into something new all right, but no one ever said that new had to be good.

Chapter Twelve

As the day approached for me to head off to school, my parents faced a reality. They weren't going to have their little girl walking five miles to school alone, and my mom sure wasn't going to make that trek. In the blistering cold of Albertan winters, it wouldn't be entirely sane of us, and besides, with all the work my mom had to do by hand around the home, an extra ten miles a day wouldn't leave her the time she needed.

Dad had worked the farm hard enough to stash a few dollars away, and my parents decided on a triple venture. First, Dad bought an additional quarter of land. Then he bought us a new car – a 1949 Meteor, two-tone green. The thing was a beaut, as far as I was concerned. All I had experienced until that time was travel by horse wagon or sleigh. I could stand on the floor and not hit my head on the ceiling. That, and the fact of fast travel protected from the elements are mainly what I remember, besides the one more important point. It allowed us to move off the farm.

We moved on into town, just a quarter mile from the school. We sold off the horses and cows, bringing just some chickens along with us for eggs. Dad was also able to modernize a bit by then, getting himself a John Deere tractor and some other machinery. Yes, things were looking up for the Novak family. And not just financially.

See, with the move into town, we had a bigger home at last, and between that and school, I suddenly faced something I wasn't quite sure what to do with, space. Space between my mom and me. I finally had my own room and this home had a separate kitchen and living room – imagine! There was still no indoor plumbing, so we got to enjoy the continued thrill of walking to the outhouse all summer and winter long. So now, the only question left was what to do with this newfound freedom.

It's worth pointing a few things out here. First, I was only six years old when we moved and as I got ready to enter school. It's easy enough to talk about freedom from a constantly vigilant mother whose ready tongue spoke for me and more or less shut my own initiative down. But at age six all I felt was dull sensation that something was wrong, that I needed some time to myself if only to reflect.

Second, that absence of time for reflection, coupled probably with a mind too young to think otherwise, meant that I longed to please my mother. She was my measure of all things, and it hadn't yet occurred to me that she was measuring me always by the ghost of a perfect child. A stern look if I laughed out loud didn't yet mean to me, Must you be so loud? At age six, it meant,

Proper young ladies do not laugh out loud. You do wish to be a proper lady, don't you? And I did, for her.

My mother could sing beautifully. She took part in the community choir and sang around home when she was in the mood. Wanting to be like her, wanting to please her, I took to singing. At first I would sing on my own, in my room, practicing on the songs I had heard her singing. But finally one day, I wanted to show how much I could be like her, so I sang for her a song I'd heard her sing while scrubbing the dishes or washing the clothes. Mother raised one magnificent eyebrow and looked my way. "What is that, Irene? Singing? You have no voice at all, do you? Must get that from your father. He's completely tone deaf too. Please, if you're going to sing, do it in your own room. No need to make us all listen." Ugh! I was destroyed! But I wished to please her and that was always the final matter, so I vowed to stop singing at home from then on, even though I found myself with some talent for singing in my adult years.

Third, the grass was not at all greener on the other side. I cherished new freedom most of all because I was headed off to school, but I learned that having mother nearby – very much as when I was dragged to my cousins' home – was an asset rather than the liability it felt to be. Damn divine order and its wily ways!

The school was tiny, because the town was tiny. It was just two rooms, harboring the first to third grades and the fourth to eighth. The cousin who was my age, who helped his siblings in torturing me, entered school at the same time and as the two of us stared at the school room, we were terrified. If I had any sense of relief for myself, it was to see him as scared as I. If I had ever felt justice in my life to that point, it was also to see him as scared as I.

My mother had walked me to school, of course, as she would every day the first year. The first day she spoke for a moment with the teacher and just as when my dad and Mr. Beckerman spoke, I didn't get one word. They spoke in English. That was how the whole school day would be. I didn't know a lick of the language, except how to spell my name.

As I sat that first day in school, my entire mission was to hold back the tears. Mouths were moving, sounds were made, but I hadn't a clue what was going on. I saw things written on a chalkboard, and I saw the other children reacting to things the teacher said. And I felt absolutely dumb.

When we had time for recess, I was alone. My cousin and I spoke Ukrainian, but I wasn't too keen on hanging out with someone who took pleasure in torturing me. We passed some words from time to time, but for the most part I watched as the children formed playgroups. And as English came to me over the months, I learned one terrible fact. Those playgroups were early cliques. If you weren't in, you weren't in. Some of the groups formed around lifestyle and religion and the rest formed around that kind of security people want to feel in a large group. Once that security is found, it is hard to let it go. After I learned to communicate with the kids, I realized that I was, in a sense, excommunicated before I had ever joined, because I had never joined. Having always been with my Mom, having never really interacted with other kids who didn't try to look at me while I was using the outhouse, I didn't know how to break into those cliques. I didn't really know how to be a friend or make a friend at all.

My cousin fared a little better than I. I'm not sure if it's because he was a boy or because he was more aggressive and could and would more push himself into group. Or maybe, because he was happy to help the other kids harass me, which became something of a playground pastime, though less drastic than what I faced at my cousins' house.

The childhood dream of buying a dress was virtually extinguished because I knew now what that involved, at least with my mom. But each day at school, that secret hope tried surging back to life because many of the girls did wear Bo Peep dresses. They seldom wore pants. I wanted to wear store-bought dresses and try fitting in, or to wear pants and at least be comfortable while I didn't fit in! Either would be an improvement, I was sure. I knew the money wasn't there for the first choice, and the option wasn't there for the second. "I'm not raising a boy," Mom told me, and those five words ended the conversation forever.

All the while, I did have a single pair of pants – dark brown, wool pants with straps at the bottom of the legs. And they were too short. Still, I was so sick of dresses, I always looked forward to my chance to use them on the coldest days of the year. When the wind chill hit 40 below zero, Mom grumbled a little and handed me the pants without a word. I knew I wasn't supposed to show my delight. After all, I did want to be a proper lady. That's how Mom was raising me, and the more I realized that she was my only real support, the more I needed her.

So my first taste of freedom – life without Mom, meant loneliness and harassment, just as it had when we visited my cousins. I began to think the ill sort of negative feeling I had about being attached to Mom at the hip was the wrong kind of feeling to have. She wanted the best for me, I was starting to see. She wanted me to grow into a lady of the highest caliber, and here I had thought I should be able to have more space and be more expressive. But I saw that space did not bring acceptance, and maybe, after all, one should not express too much. "A proper lady does not speak out of turn," my Mother had told me. And although it seemed to me that my Mom spoke an awful lot when we were with others, I guessed that it wasn't out of turn and that she already knew and lived by the Law of Inexpression. I resolved, by the end of first grade, that I would renew my efforts to make my mother proud of me, and happy. I resolved that I would say less and watch more, to learn from the things she did around the house. If I could achieve all this with her, then someday, I was sure, I would find a man whom I could also please. To hell with the kids at school. I was going to find a way to be loved.

Chapter Thirteen

Proper ladies were apparently not supposed to speak out of turn, but as far as I could tell, Sunday either dismissed the rule, or all of Sunday was "in turn."

My parents were not all that religious except for their quirky beliefs surrounding God's anger. I mean, we were Ukrainian Greek Orthodox by name, but what is it to say you're part of a religion if you don't generally participate in that religion and if it doesn't really change the way you live? Being baptized into a faith doesn't mean much one way or another. Saying you are Catholic or Buddhist or Greek Orthodox when you don't live by the faith is a totally empty claim. Then there are people who live by a faith, and they're the ones who really have a right to say they're part of the faith. And finally, there are those who live by a faith and want to force everyone else to live by that same faith, paradoxically neglecting the faith they claim to live, since the whole concept of love generally goes right out the window

The thing about our church was that there wasn't really one. We had a priest who would swing by a few times a year to give sermons and to baptize children that were born in his absence and that was the sum of my baptized faith. But that didn't mean we never went to church.

Well, this is where it gets funny, because it makes you want to laugh about the people who say you have to go to church every Sunday. To me, church was a lot of large bottoms. I mean that literally. When our priest wasn't in town, we would attend a Ukrainian Catholic church that was all of 500 square feet total. Even that congregation only met once a month, because they relied on a traveling priest as well.

Fine. We were going to church once a month. But since we weren't Catholics, we were relegated to the back of the room. All the Catholics stayed up front and took Communion during the mass. So what did that mean for a child? The size of the church meant that we were all packed together like *proverbial* sardines. There wasn't room for chairs, so we were all on our feet for the entire mass. My parent's faith put me at the back of the church. And my height meant that I spent the entire time looking at some adult's rear end. Believe me, if there was anything that made me realize that traditional faith was a little nuts, this was it.

But it got worse. If English would have been hard enough for me to follow, they didn't even give me that. The whole sermon was in Latin, which meant even as I learned English, not one thing made sense to me at church. I honestly didn't get why we went until I realized that Sunday was not so much about learning from the Bible. I noticed that the men from both faiths spent much of the sermon outside, in front of the church talking. And that the women joined in their own little female gaggles afterwards and added to the talk. If no one knew Latin and half the people weren't paying attention anyway, what was Sunday but a social event? This was a big clue for me about the way things worked.

There was something else, though. Another single event that put a whole new spin on church and religion for me. That's when the Baptists came to town.

And this is where I have to pause. This is where I have to comment. Because in this day and age, it's important that we start to take a hard look at religion. A rational look, which is key, because a lot of people either want to promote their own religion or tear religions down. That kind of polarization is exactly what turns people against people and religion against religion. It's what makes us forget that at the core of any religion or spirituality in general is supposed to be one principle, and that is love.

So when we take a look at religion, we have to do two things at the same time, we have to notice where it's done us good, and we have to see where it's done us ill. When I say the Baptists came to town, and that this turned our town upside down, that is a truth. But then, you've got two groups ready to react. One group says, "Yeah, those darn Baptists." And another that says, "Wait a second – are you really going to make a generalization about Baptists? Are you really going to paint them as the bad guys?"

The fact is, every religion out there teaches love. There's nothing wrong with that underlying faith. It's just that sometimes, people within a religion forget that, or think they're acting from love when they're acting from ego, wanting everyone in the world to believe just as they do. There aren't any bad guys in this story. But there was an event where I learned a lot about religion, and how crazy it can make people. And like I said, that event was when the Baptists came to town.

They were missionaries, those Baptists. They were ready to have everyone in town believe as they did, and they were fanatics about their job. They would visit people's homes and try to show them where their church had failed them, where the teachings were skewed, or where people were not living with the zeal that the Lord God was supposed to give them. And that, after all, was proof of a fallen religion. But join the Baptists, see, and you too would be filled with the Holy Ghost.

Or something to that effect. It was very strange to me because I'd never been filled with any Holy Ghost. And I wasn't quite sure what zeal was. But the argument was a strong one because the missionaries were obviously so sure of their faith and of its holy fire that other people wanted to feel it too. So in time, some people in the community were ready to convert.

It was a big to-do for such a little community, and the event took place on the river. Most the people from the community came, even though about quarter were getting baptized into the new faith. The rest were there either in morbid curiosity or in a state of raw desperation, wanting to save their friends and family from this terrible mistake. If I had been older, I might have been among this second group, because down in line, alongside the river, were my grandparents, several aunts, an uncle, and their families.

This day was another instance of my learning that freedom wasn't such a positive thing, because among the crowds gathered by the river, I got separated from my mom and dad. I wandered along the river bank, avoiding the line of people waiting to walk into the water for submersion and baptism. I began looking with some desperation for my parents, because I could feel the tension of the scene. I heard cursing behind me and turned to see a man yelling at the Baptists. "You leave my mother alone!" he screamed. "Mother, get out of there for Christ's sake! What are you doing? We don't need any goddamned Baptists in this family. Don't you go under that water. Don't you …"

His cursing didn't do the job. The woman went under, then came back up again with her hands lifted to the heavens. "Hallelujah!" she proclaimed. "Hallelujah, it's time the Lord's light shined into our family. Praise the Lord!"

"Mother, for the last time – *get out!* We don't need any goddamned light!"

I don't know if I understood it all, but I heard more and more arguments starting to break out. And then, I saw it. Oh, the embarrassment. Maybe that's why the man was yelling. But as the first women climbed back up to shore from their baptism, it was plain as day. You could see their breasts through their wet shirts. The shame, the awfulness of the situation. It was all I could do to keep from crying for them. Showing your breasts was unacceptable. I knew, because in my home we didn't even talk about breasts or anything having to do with sex, and for all my years under my parents' roof, we never would. If ever Mom had to refer to a woman's body (because, after all, my dad never would), she would refer to "the chest" and "down there."

When I saw the women that day arriving on shore, for all intents and purposes naked, I understood why these Baptist missionaries were so controversial. I understood why people were yelling, and now, I was really scared. Where *were* my mom and dad? I had to get out of there. It dawned on me why we were there in the first place – my aunt was going to get baptized. Mom and Dad must have been there to stop her from showing her breasts. I made my way closer to the line of people waiting for submersion, and sure enough, there was Mom talking with my aunt. But as I approached, I didn't hear her saying anything about my aunt's "chest" and the horror it would mean for our family if she soaked her shirt like the rest of the women. Nor was she at all frantic in her tone. It was more like a robot tone, coldly, rationally explaining the situation. "It isn't that you shouldn't make your own choice," she pointed out. "It's just that we can do without fanaticism. Look around yourself and what do you see? You see people with time to be preached at and to be scorned for not spending their every waking minute with the Bible? These people are here to survive. That's their focus. That has to be their focus."

"That is the very problem," said my aunt. "Everyone's so caught up in survival, they forget why they're surviving. The brothers said that God takes care of all the birds, so he'll take care of people too, because we're more valuable than birds. God won't let anything bad happen to the faithful."

Mom shook her head, hardly believing what she heard. "God lets bad things happen to people of faith all the time. You go worship God all day long if you want, but come winter, don't come begging at our door for food when you didn't bother spending your days working."

"It won't matter," said my aunt. "I'd rather starve and be in God's good graces than to live like a king or a queen here on earth."

"Yes," said my mom. "That's what we're living like here. Kings and queens." She looked down and saw me, took me by the hand and walked off.

Even more curious, though, was my father, who was talking to his brother with all the animation I had expected to see in my mom. I didn't get it. Did it really matter if people could see my uncle's chest? Mom was dragging me from the scene with a determined pace so I only caught a few words from the argument between my dad and uncle.

"… so *stubborn!*" said my dad.

True to his third-child nature of blending into the background and preferring time alone, Dad was not generally outspoken at all. My mouth was gaping just a little as I watched him, till Mom clamped shut my jaw. "Young ladies do not stare and do not let their mouths hang open," she told me.

"… laziest people … give a *damn* about God!" yelled my uncle as I turned to catch a last glimpse of the argument. "And I mean to do something about it. … going to raise these people up and make them *care* again."

And that was the last I heard. At least for the time. Mom got me to the car and we waited there in silence till Dad showed up. I'd never seen him so red. But he didn't say a word as he approached us and we all got in the car and drove home, silent as death. I didn't really get how this would affect our family for the rest of my life. I didn't even get what was going on between my dad and uncle. But it would all make sense to me the following year. And I would find myself disgusted.

Chapter Fourteen

After a year of school and a year of being generally harassed by the other kids, I was beginning to understand English. In some cases, this made harassment worse, each time it dawned on me what the kids were saying. They taunted me as being stupid for not knowing how to speak, while I was learning an entire language. They taunted me for being different because I didn't even know how to play games, which seemed a given since no one could give me the rules in Ukrainian. And they taunted me for being weird because I never hung out with the others – another matter of victim by language at first, and then of the cliques that formed while I was still learning English.

But all of that was fine, because most of my time was spent with my mother, and since mother spoke my mind, and her words often showed how useless I was at anything I put my hand to, I had developed a distinctive talent for burying myself deep inside. These silly children's chants and taunts could hardly touch me. They were nothing beside the humiliation that came from my own flesh and blood. I would go about my work at school, then get home as quickly as I could. There, at least, I always felt hope that I could some day live up to Mother's dreams for me and could get her approval rather than disdain.

During my second school year, the Baptists erected a small building and began their weekly worship and more frequent Bible readings. This had a twofold impact on me. First, I had more room between me and the butt in front of me when I attended church because some of the population no longer attended the Catholic church. And second, there was a sudden and definite rift formed between our family and my uncle's family – unfortunately, not the cousins who excelled at torturing me. It was another of dad's brothers, who wasn't kidding when he told my dad that he was going to do something about the spiritual community. He became the Baptist preacher for the town as the missionaries headed on to their work elsewhere.

My parents wouldn't attend, but because my uncle was preaching and my grandparents attended, I wanted to see what it was all about. For whatever reason, my parents let me go. Maybe they knew what I would find.

My first surprise was that my uncle was thunder and lightning. I was intrigued by some of the stories he read. There seemed to be some cool magic in that Bible! But I didn't understand much of what followed. I knew it was important, because there was a lot of screaming and finger wagging. I sort of hoped he would wag his finger right at me, because maybe that was some kind of Baptist blessing, but he never did. It was more of a general wagging, and I figured he was casting a blessing onto all the people. I even started to think that words like "Sodom and Gomorrah" were the Baptist version of "Abracadabra."

After my uncle read from the holy book and gave his sermon, there was a period when he would go through the congregation and ask each person how many verses they had read from the Bible that week. Apparently, reading a lot of verses made you a very good person and this intrigued me a great deal. I was not accustomed to receiving compliments, but they seemed to be very nice things to receive. The people who read a lot were heartily commended. So one week, I resolved to read as much as I could from the Bible and come to church and make a difference. I wanted to be known as the little girl with a heart of gold, the girl whom the community had a new respect for because she was so truly devoted to God.

It was a struggle for me to read anything at all, since I was still learning English. But I was getting pretty good at it by the beginning of second grade. I could speak it pretty well and could read a little. I marched proudly into the church the following Sunday and was so excited I couldn't focus at all on the story or anything that followed until they came to the congregation for their numbers. I heard a few adults give their numbers and they were higher than mine, but of course they were adults and they should have read more. I wanted to be the first kid to give her number, and I was. My uncle called on me and I said proudly to my feet. "This week, I read three whole verses."

And then, incredible! My uncle rolled his eyes and looked to the next person, as if he was ashamed of my proclamation. I didn't know what to think. I didn't know what to do. But I sat uncomfortably, wondering if I had really seen what I thought I saw.

A moment more and the congregation forgot about me completely, and by that point I was glad. My uncle was calling on my grandfather and I was forgotten in the uproar. He read more than 800 verses of the Bible in just that week. Oh, the commendations, the congratulations, the shoulder-patting was incredible. And amidst it all, I turned my eyes downward and knew once more that my input was not needed, that my efforts were not appreciated. No wonder my mother thought for me and spoke for me – she was protecting me from this unkind reality. I knew then that I would not return to this church. I would find my place beside my mom and, more and more, try to do as a good girl should.

Chapter Fifteen

Even if church was bad news, I still learned a thing or two. Mom had already taught me a few things from the Bible. She said the very first story was all about how a man and woman got in trouble and had to leave paradise because they were naked. That fit with how shameful I knew it was to be naked. But we learned about other things too. For instance, when God was angry with me for stealing a cookie and ruined our crops with a hailstorm, that was nothing. Apparently He did much worse when He really got ticked off. There were all sorts of plagues, including deaths of newborns. And He even killed one guy just for touching His Ark of the Covenant. Mom and Dad were right, God was pretty easy to make angry.

There was a list of stuff you never did unless you wanted God angry, which obviously would be a stupid thing to want. There were Ten Commandments. There were so many rules in the Bible, I knew I would never learn them all. But ten seemed like a pretty reasonable number, especially since some were pretty much common sense. I didn't know what it meant to covet, but I learned that "bearing false witness" meant lying. Killing was straightforward and so was stealing. I knew that one from the hailstorm anyway.

At home, I had to deal with an apparent contradiction. I knew that Mom and Dad didn't want anymore hailstorms, yet somehow, they seemed willing to do away with some of this list. Lying and stealing were never encouraged by word, but they were by deed.

Mom often lived in her own reality and seemed to make up facts about how we lived and who we were as a family. "You know, Irene," she would tell me, "no one really needs to know that I make your dresses here at home. I know the girls at school are wearing things bought from the stores. But your dresses are just as nice. You can tell them yours are from the store as well."

It was one of the things she knew I was teased about from time to time. The next time the kids harassed me for wearing "mamma clothes," I said I didn't know what they were talking about. My dresses were straight from Bo Peep. "Oh yeah? Where are the tags?" they demanded. I said I didn't like tags so I took them off. "Mamma clothes, mamma clothes, lies about her dresses!" they chanted. So I was more miserable than before.

A lot of lies circled around the family as a whole. We had Baptist family members, we had physical abuse and neglect within the family and plenty more family secrets. I was told precisely how to deny things or explain them away, and this was presented as the right thing to do. Even when my cousins physically injured me, Mom was in her own world of denial and make-believe. "Irene, we both know how clumsy you can be. For heaven's sake, you *must* stop trying to pin it on your cousins every time they are good enough to have us over. Don't you go telling other people that your cousins are causing you a problem. You look them right in the eye and let them know that you hurt yourself. You'll feel a whole lot better making sure they know."

For years I did exactly as I was told and felt miserable every time I had to lie. I didn't know what Mom meant by feeling better. I also had this hidden fear that God was building up some fantastic punishment to exact on me. I was lying all the time and not seeing any immediate results. I wondered when He would get me for what I was doing. The surprising thing was that my dad always preached honesty, yet he never stopped my mom from her fantasy world and lies and he never stopped her from telling me how to lie. It was all very confusing in the end.

Then, of course, there was stealing, which I was strictly forbidden from doing. Yet, one night when he wasn't expected home and Mom was having a sewing circle in the living room, Dad came in quietly with a gunny sack and snuck the thing down into the cellar. Later, when all the women cleared out, Dad brought the sack upstairs again and dumped out a bunch of fresh apples and oranges.

This was an extraordinary treat. Normally during the winter the only time we got fresh fruit was when my parents bought a box of Clementines for Christmas. The Clementines were a double bonus. First, they tasted great and were incredibly refreshing amidst a long winter of preserved foods. Second, Clementines came wrapped in green tissue paper, and this was almost nicer than the oranges themselves. This tissue paper was the nicest toilet paper we would have all year – far better than the newspapers and catalogue pages we usually had to use! So fresh fruit, in any event, was a premium.

Much as that was the case, my dad had to sneak this sack of fruit into the house for a reason, it was stolen. Nobody needed to say a thing. We all understood. But for me, this was a classic example of mixed messages. I was told I shouldn't steal, but I was shown that it was okay. This tied in with the lying thing too, or rather, not telling the truth. I was told that I shouldn't mention to anyone that he'd brought the fruit home. "Now Irene," said my mother, "we've got a very special treat here, but it's really only special if we keep it to ourselves. So don't you go blabbing around town about this fine fruit we've got, or next time you wouldn't get any and you'll have to sit and watch us eat it all."

Their example played out through my own actions twice. Some years later I would receive twenty-five cents a week and would spend it on candy with a friend. One day I saw fifty cents in a cupboard and I grabbed it. I spent the whole amount on candy and later insisted that I didn't know where it disappeared to. It was a good chance to practice both stealing and lying together.

Another time I took something from a store. The store display showed this red scarf with a suit and I took both into the dressing room to try them on. They looked great. I promptly stuffed the scarf into my purse, purchased the suit, and left the store. Later, I felt so guilty about the scarf that I never wore it, and threw it out years later to have it off my mind. Luckily, it never did leave my mind. I knew that I never wanted to steal again, even if it seemed okay by my parents' example.

The funny thing is that we all know we're not supposed to lie. We all know we're not supposed to steal. But plenty of people do both. I often wonder whether they know how paradoxical and confusing it is for kids. I wonder if they realize how often that mixed message backfires against them. I mean, I only stole once from my parents, but I lied often. Worst of all, the more it happened, the more I came to distrust them and to feel as if I should distance myself from them and ignore the things they said. The irony with my mom is that she wanted so much to be my only great influence yet the way she and Dad were, I couldn't keep fitting their words and actions in with my intuitive sense of a trustworthy parent. So it's not much wonder why I began lying to them, hiding my true self from them and over time, needing to rebel.

Chapter Sixteen

In the following years of school, the other kids didn't become particularly more kind, but as my English improved, they backed off to a degree. I did have friends, but for a long time, those friends lived in our attic at home.

For most kids, school is as much a social excursion as it is a drudgery of learning, much the way church is for most adults. For me, it couldn't be both because I had no friends. So when second grade began and I found that things were more or less the same as always, I decided on a different option than school. I decided to stay at home and be with my friends.

I had invented these friends over the summer, maybe because I had learned from school what friends were, and wished that I could have some of my own. My companions, though, were nothing more than boxes in the attic that I stacked up and dressed in my clothes. Good enough. A child's imagination can stretch and create realities of almost anything. I had names for every friend. I spent time dressing them as other children would their dolls. I would have tea parties or play house, or whatever else seemed most fun at the time. And I tell you now, those boxes moved and spoke with me, I am sure.

There may have been a reason it all became that real, besides some special psychological explanation about my need to connect with people on equal terms. Mom did everything around the house by hand and that meant making wine as well. This she did in the attic, and I being so bright as I was, had a special spoon hidden in among my box-friends, and from time to time, I would sample the concoction to test its progress. Moving and talking boxes? No great mystery there.

In any case, that is where I would spend my days, rather than going to school. Why not? I was only learning about discrimination at school. I was learning communication, albeit a sort of twisted form given my circumstance, at home. Perhaps this was my first sign of rebellion. It had to manifest at some point, because there was just too much being repressed.

Except I wasn't rebelling. At least, not to any critical extent. My *modus operandi* was still to watch my mom and follow her indications. As far as I could see, education was not important and was not to be taken too seriously. She and Dad had only finished third grade. They never paid attention to what I was learning in school and they did not help with my homework. The only real assistance they gave, and this was in fact very helpful, was to start speaking primarily in English inside our home. They seemed to realize that it would be helpful for me to know what my teachers were saying.

But the primary message I received was that school was not critical and since school was such a bad experience as it was turning out to be, it didn't seem to me that I ought to bother. Couple that with the fact that the truth did not seem highly prized in my household, I began to fabricate. I'd tell Mom that we had the day off, or the afternoon off, or the week off – whatever suited me. That approach lasted precisely until my report card showed up with dozens of absences. My mom put a quick end to my games in the attic and it was back to school for me.

School might have continued to be horrible except for one thing, I finally formed a friendship that grew with a girl named Margie – a girl who would literally transform my understanding of and approach to everything.

You say the word "everything" and you're bound to get yourself in trouble. It's easy to exaggerate. But if someone can dramatically shift your point of view, then the whole world around you really *does* change. And if the whole world changes, then you have to interact with it differently.

Our meeting was strange. My motives at that moment are still completely hidden to me. Maybe there was some hidden spiritual tie between Margie and me that prompted my actions. Maybe it was just the thrill of "what if?" But, during the spring of my second grade, I saw Margie leaning out through a school window. My entire view consisted of her back end and her legs.

A kid. Leaning out the window. Completely vulnerable. Was it years of things pent up even in my oh-so-young self? *What if I just ....*

And yes, I really did. I ran up behind her and pushed and out the window she fell, directly onto her head! I looked out in horror as I realized what was unfolding. Her face went pale and I expect mine did too. Had I pushed someone from a window? My mind started racing. What would happen? Would I get in trouble? Would she go to the hospital? Would she *die?* I knew what happened if someone's neck was broken, and it's all I could envision.

Margie seemed to suddenly shake it off, sitting up in a daze. I couldn't believe my luck, but it seemed that she was fine! I pulled my head back in the window and went about my business hoping that no one saw what happened. And no one had, unless you counted my conscience, which after a few days I could no longer ignore. It made me miserable, replaying over and over what I'd done. So I decided to approach Margie and let courage take its course.

I approached during recess, but found that my courage was out the window in a flash. All too appropriate. I couldn't fess up to what I'd done, but somehow we got to talking. And that afternoon, Margie, one of the few kids who never seemed to bend to the playground will, became my friend.

This posed a little problem, because Margie was the girl who had lived next door when we lived in our first house. She was from the "Ukrainian Catholic" group so our parents had nothing to do with one another. That fact would naturally pit Mom against our friendship at least in the early going and I would just have to see whether Margie could win her over. The good Lord knows that Margie won me over quickly enough. Of course, how hard could that be in the case of someone without any friends? But Margie proved to be much more than a bottom-of-the-barrel option.

Of course, first things first. I had to figure out what it meant to have a real friend – something I hadn't experienced before. That meant actually communicating with a person and not just my boxes. In the early going that was a struggle because it was too strange a notion for me to speak my mind. Margie, though, was the truest of friends and it was always clear that she wanted to hear from me. So slowly, over months, I learned to open my mouth and let the words come out. And this felt good. It felt right. And as the words came more freely, plenty of my old thoughts resurfaced. I had always felt that something was wrong when I was taught *not* to speak when I was taught that someone else ought to decide things for me and speak my mind, which was *not* my mind. Experience had shown me often that Mom was right – the world did not care for my input. The more I saw that, the more I felt that not speaking was the best thing for me the more I felt that I ought to hide behind my mom and let life do its thing. The feeling that I should speak my mind had to be buried because it didn't find any support in real life.

Until Margie. Until I did find a voice and discovered that it was appreciated by a friend. Until I found that there was value in what I had to offer. Then, the old thoughts and feelings resurfaced and I began to wonder why Mom never let me express who I was and what I wished. This new reality was the birth, so to speak, of a new Irene – one I hadn't seen before and many people probably wish had never been born. But it was inevitable that this Irene be born, because someone else had been born – Alexander. And even though I spent my days trying to be the perfect child, living out the archetype of child number one, I simply couldn't do it – because I was child number two.

Chapter Seventeen

I planned to run away for about a week. I waited for something to set it off. I could only follow through if I was good and angry. And one day, Mom gave me the needed ammunition. "Mamma, can I go over to Margie's?"

I remember seeing as if it were slow motion. The whole thing is still clear, because I played the scene a hundred times in my head as I stole away from my home. She looked over to me, one eyebrow raised. "Irene, you are spending too much time with this Margie girl. Ukrainian Catholics – I mean, who are they to spend time with. It's a poor influence, Irene. I don't like it. Time for you to remember who your family is. No one outside this home takes care of you. I take care of you and I hardly see your face inside this home anymore. I think it's time we give this Margie thing a rest for a while. Give it a week, then we'll see whether you can visit Margie."

"But Mamma …"

"And where under the heavens have you learned this tone of voice? Is this what school is teaching you these days – to argue with me? If that's what education is, it's something we don't need any more of in this household." She turned, muttering to herself, "Rolling over in my grave already, the way this girl talks back." And she went to cutting up carrots for our dinner salad.

It wasn't much of anything, but it was the sum of all things, and it was enough to push me out my bedroom window with a small bag over my shoulder. The bag had a single change of clothes and my toothbrush – no toothpaste. I made my way carefully to the road so that my mom wouldn't see me through the windows and I started off at a hefty pace for my short little legs.

It is a very long road ahead of you when you don't know where you're going. Without a goal, there is only the road stretching beyond where you can see, and you know that it never ends because there is no one or any shelter at the end. It gave me time to think, and at this precious little age, something occurred to me. My parents fought a lot at home. My father was not a weak man, yet my mother wanted to dominate everything. So they would butt heads because, although Dad let her have her own way with me, he would not let her have it with him. He didn't care if she lied about things, that was just the way Mom was. But he wouldn't let her tell him how to be. So he raised his voice and she raised her own, because each wished to win the decibel battle. And I would creep off to my room wondering why they argued so much.

On this day when I ran from home, it occurred to me that they could be yelling about me. God had gotten angry with me just for stealing a single cookie, and He was probably a lot nicer than Mom and Dad. It probably didn't take anything at all to make them furious with me and maybe that's why they were so angry with each other too. Maybe running away wasn't just the best for me. Maybe it was best for the entire family. Maybe they could get back to the way I thought moms and dads were supposed to be, actually enjoying each other and getting along.

Even worse, the kids at school treated me badly and my cousins treated me badly. Maybe I just wasn't cut out for making people happy. Maybe I wasn't cut out for being around others. Did it make the most sense just to be gone? Would running away do the trick?

I made it a good quarter of a mile with those thoughts zipping about my brain before seeing our car pull out of the driveway. I was immediately relieved. I hadn't a clue where I was headed, and didn't know what I would do about dinner. I stopped and watched the car driving my way, more relieved with each moment that Mom was coming to get me. Stupid, stupid, stupid! I thought. Mom does take care of me, and I always forget that when I go somewhere without her, I feel lost. Stupid – I should never run away from home. At least now I can just go home and watch her cut the carrots.

But stupid wasn't the word for running away. Stupid was the word for my relief. If Mom belittled me all my life for not doing things as she expected, if she spoke on my behalf and made all my choices for me, it was at least easy for me to retreat and become myself somewhere deep inside my body. But I didn't face belittling when my mom got me home from my short stint outdoors. I didn't face her telling me it was wrong or explaining that she was looking out for my best interest. I faced a mom I had never seen before, a mom who had become violent because, over the months, I had begun to question her authority. So as we walked indoors, to my complete surprise, she threw me onto our couch, picked me up by my feet and beat my butt red. She was screaming as I'd never heard her scream before. I was screaming as I'd never heard myself scream before. And the beating went on and on until I could no longer stand and she could no longer hold me up.

I whimpered. I crawled. And I made it slowly to my room. And my back end throbbed and throbbed. It would be swollen and bruised for days. As I lay on my floor in a panic, that was the hour. It was the hour when I knew that I must get away for real. Mom left no question about whether she was my protector or my controller. The sooner I could leave home, the better it would be.

Chapter Eighteen

That was beating number one. It introduced me to an entirely new notion about how life worked. Often, I had felt defeated in more subtle ways and these had led me to question my mother in the first place. But beating me till my butt was raw, that was entirely new. Upon reflection, it might not have been so different from the many times I had *played*, as it was called at my cousins' home. When my mother saw what I suffered over there, generally bruises across my body, she said nothing and she did nothing. And it was always curious to me, as if this was somehow perfectly natural for a little girl to go through as part of her initiation into life. For all I knew, that was the case. I had nothing to compare it to all those years. And on instances when my clothes were torn because of sexual abuse and harassment, I was chastised. If I tried to explain, I was told not to pass blame for my carelessness. "A real lady doesn't speak badly of other people," Mom told me. "She learns to avoid those situations that will get her dirty." So the blame, I learned, was my own.

All of that was an era of my lifetime I might proclaim *the subtle years*. These were days when things felt wrong, but I accepted them as normal and therefore right. The day my mother beat me, there was no longer anything about her that was subtle. She stood revealed, most especially because the beating was not in the heat of the moment, as it might have been in the midst of an argument. No, she had picked me up, driven me home in utter silence, walked me into the house, then threw me to the couch and began the rampage. That was a punishment thought through.

In many ways, this broke open a new world for my mother as well. Had she continued thinking me so fragile that I might be lost from this world, she couldn't have thought to beat me. But there was another issue brewing, and it must have driven the violence.

Her fear of losing me had kept her physically in check all these years, but now, as I had begun to challenge her with simple questions, her fear shifted from the physical to the emotional. Was it possible that she would lose a second child, only this time in the heart and mind? Would I reject her as a mother and essentially disappear from her life? It was this fear that must have driven to new madness. And the more distant I became, the more this fear must have controlled her very thoughts because the day I ran away was just the beginning.

In months to follow, I withdrew more and more because I didn't recognize who I was living with. I was afraid, because I did not know how to be. "What is this, Irene?" she would ask me. "I work day and night for you. You're the only thought in my mind. And you've got to spend your days pouting. What kind of child do you think hides from her mother the way you do? Have you got any notion how selfish you're being? Do you even think about helping out around the home? No. Everything is for you, isn't it Irene?"

She played on something else, too. School was such a difficult environment for me because of the kids, I had a hard time focusing on my work. I would end up bringing it home and trying to do it there, but Mom and Dad had third grade eductions. I was already at their educational level so they could not help with my homework. What's more, they wouldn't even try. "You want to spend your time with all of that, that's fine," said my Mother. "But I've got no end to work here and I'm not about to spend my time on that nonsense."

So my grades suffered and Mom and Dad really couldn't care about that when reports cards showed up. However, as Mom grew more bitter, grades became an issue when it was convenient to her. "Every day in your bedroom. Every night in your bedroom. Won't even help me with the dinner. I assume it's because you've got homework, so I give you all the time you need. But you don't bother learning a thing, do you? Dumb as a log, and stubborn too, aren't you? Just like your father. You'll grow up to marry some local farmer, and you think school learning is going to mean a thing? No. Help out around the house, you'll learn what you need to survive. That kind of learning will put all your days of school to shame."

So I would make an attempt or two to help out, but even in third grade, would deviate slightly from the way Mom thought a thing must be done. I would make an error, or not, but still Mom would steal back the work, then scold me for being lazy and incompetent. So I would sulk back to my room until she brought the issue up again.

My dad noticed the obvious shift going on between my mother and me, but as far as I know, he never learned why. Raising me was Mom's duty, just as driving to the farm every day and bringing home money for food was his. Mom had no place in telling him what crops to plant, or where. Neither did he feel it necessary or appropriate to comment on my condition. So I would see him looking at me sometimes during dinner, as if to figure out just who that was sitting near the end of the table. And when he couldn't figure it out, he'd stab his fork into a potato and go back to his dinner, deciding he would decipher me some other time. If it ever became important.

In the early months of third grade, as I realized I was on my own for schooling and I wanted to spend as much time away from Mom as I could, I found myself venturing outdoors on the weekends. By now I was at least allowed out of sight and I made my way a whole lot further from home that my mother ever knew. I doubted if she cared, because after she beat me, she was probably not supremely concerned with my safety.

There was a reason I started venturing so far and it had to do with babies. My parents always wanted to avoid the subject of sex, or even the topic of boys and girls in general. And if you think about it, it must have been a challenge to raise a kid on a farm and not have to broach those issues. Maybe that was an added benefit for Mom and Dad of moving me into town. There were still farms all around us, though, and it's amazing that I never actually saw a cow giving birth. It sure would have brought up questions!

But I knew that cows had calves somehow. I knew that people had babies. And it started to dawn on me that it was very strange these things would so suddenly show up. How did they get there? So one day when I was in third grade, I asked my mom how cows got calves. "They find them underneath trees," she told me.

This was a great revelation. I didn't think she would volunteer so much information. Because if that's how a cow found a calf, it had to be how women found their babies. I thought it would be a great idea to have a baby brother or sister in the house so I would have someone to play with and take care of. This would give me someone to be with when I wanted to avoid my mom. So I started wandering into the woods around the town in the afternoons, hoping to stumble onto a child.

I learned which trees had nooks in them across a huge area of the woods – I was checking inside for babies. I learned every bend of the path that ran through the woods and I got to know the deer paths and hiding spots, based on areas of depressed grasses behind bushes and beneath low-hanging trees. But I never found a baby.

I decided to ask my Mom again. She had volunteered this first information so easily, maybe she would yield a little more. I approached her one Saturday morning and said it simply: "Mom, how do the cows know which trees to look under for their calves."

Mom looked confused for a minute, then understood my question. "They find a spot beneath a tree and cough up the baby." My eyes grew wide with the notion – just imagine what *that* was like, coughing up a baby!

"Thanks Mom." She smiled and shook her head, and I walked slowly outdoors to conceal my excitement. Then I raced to the woods, found a cozy spot beneath a tree, and spent half an hour coughing.

Nothing. Not even a tiny baby. I'd have been happy with even a doll. Well, I was completely hoarse for the next hour and I stopped coughing for the day. But whenever I had the chance, I would find a different tree out in the woods, maybe you had to be under the right one, and coughed my lungs out. But I never had a baby.

I was completely discouraged, and I told Margie about what my mom had said. "Do you think it's true?"

"I don't know," Margie told me. "That doesn't seem right. I'll ask my aunt."

Margie's aunt was a Godsend. She was four years older than we were and she knew everything about how things worked. When Margie wanted to know something, that's where she went for the details. Well, the story Margie came back with was horrifying and entirely unbelievable. For the first time, we doubted her every word. "Why would people do something so shameful?" I asked. "I know my Mom and Dad don't take off their pants in front of each other. They told me how bad it would be for boys and girls to do that."

"And that whole thing about what happens to girls every month." Margie shrugged. "You ever see anything like that? It seems too weird." We agreed to be suspicious. Maybe Margie's aunt was becoming too much like other adults we knew. Margie's parents had gone so far as to say that babies came from all the love that moms and dads felt for each other, but they didn't say anything about an act so grim as sex.

For the time, we decided to leave the topic alone, and as autumn began turning to winter anyway, I wasn't in any hurry to get back into the woods. It was the season to pass time indoors, and I started hearing more and more about a brilliant way to spend the weekends indoors. It seemed that a lot of the kids at school were sleeping at each other's homes, and the notion made stars dance in my eyes. Sleeping in someone else's home meant time away from home! It meant playing with a friend all the way till bed time. From what I heard, that meant till late. I heard that some of these kids stayed up till 11:00, which was almost unthinkable, but certainly desirable. It made me wonder what 11:00 at night was like. In fact, the notion became so appealing to me over time that I made a decision. If Mom would only let me go on a sleepover, then maybe I wouldn't be so mad about the beating I got for running away. It was one of those childhood deals one makes with oneself, completely irrational, but feeding whatever is the world's most important idea at the time. Never mind that a beating was so much bigger than one choice, it was my deal with her. To myself, of course. I never told her what the deal was.

One Saturday afternoon in the fall, I approached her. "Mamma," I said, "I was wondering. …"

Mom turned around, almost surprised that I was approaching her at all. "Well, sulking one, what is it today?"

I hesitated. This was kind of a make-it-or-break-it moment, and Mom didn't know. I was ready to run and hug her. I was ready to hate her forever, or at least until I had another phenomenal request for her. "Mamma, Margie and I have been talking." My mom rolled her eyes. She kept at me about the whole *Margie thing*. She thought I was far too dependent on this friendship, and she frequently kept me from visiting Margie for a week at a time. She couldn't control the school hours so she focused on ruining my free time. "Margie asked her mom, and it's okay for me to sleep over at their house. Can I go?"

My mom set down a dish that she'd been drying and squatted down before me. "No," she said flatly. "No you can't. And do you want to know why?"

"But. …"

Mom grabbed my face roughly from beneath the chin. "I didn't ask for an argument. I asked if you want to know why." I tried to shake my head *yes* within her grip. "Because I don't like Margie. I don't like you and Margie together. You are my girl and I love you to death. Do you understand? To death. And all this girl inspires in you is some sort of hatred for me. You think I don't see that? Hmmm? You think I don't get that Margie wants to keep you away from me?" Mom shook my face in her grip. "Well I do get it. And I'm not going to let an eight year old make my own daughter hate me. I'm not." Tears were streaming down my face. "So I'm sorry that you're angry with me right now, but I can see what's best for our family. I have been here for you all your life. I'm going to keep being here, feeding you, taking care of you. Remember that. Remember I am here to love you if you will just get over this Margie. Keep spending time with her, you're going to find yourself ruining your whole life." She released her grip, patted me on the cheek, then stood and returned to her dishes.

I ran to my room. I flopped onto my bed. I cried for half an hour. Months of dreaming, and this was no sort of answer. My cheeks were still sore and that told me the answer was pretty definite. I hated her. I hated that she always got to decide.

And then I remembered that she could only decide if she were around to decide. I didn't have to hate her for that. I just had to get away so that she wasn't making my decisions. I was still pretty clear about what I got for running away the last time, but then, I didn't make much of an effort to get away last time. I had been happy to see the car, in fact, and to head back home with my mom. I wouldn't make that mistake twice. Mom was busy with dinner now. She wouldn't even have a chance to notice that I was missing for another hour. I jumped off my bed, grabbed a bag, stuffed it with as many clothes as I could and climbed out my window. Just like the first time, I was careful to get around the house so she wouldn't see me and when I made it out to the road, I ran as far as I could I ran a good five minutes, getting well past a quarter mile from the home. Then I slowed to catch my breath. No car. No Mom. I was free!

I kept walking and thinking about where I would go. It probably didn't make sense to go to Margie's, since Mom would go there first to look for me. I doubted it made sense to go to my grandparents, since she'd look there before long too. Damn. I hadn't thought this one out. The only places I knew to go, they'd either turn me back in to my mom, or she'd find me there anyway. Had to think. Had to think.

I was more than a mile from home. Still no Mom. Still no car. I started to wonder whether she would even come look. She was so frustrated with me these days, maybe it was easier to let me go. That would be great. I could just live at Margie's. Margie usually said good things about her parents. They were strict sometimes, she told me, but they let her do a lot of things too. They helped her with her homework. They always gave her time to ask questions. And they let her try her hand at lots of things around the home. That sounded great to me. Strict wasn't so bad if you got all the rest as part of the bundle. I could help out around her house and pay my way.

But I had to make sure Mom wasn't looking for me before I went there. I had to figure out a place to stay and watch. Then I'd know where to go and what to do. I could figure it all . . .

Damn, damn, and damn again! I forgot! I got so mired in figuring out all my plans. I forgot to watch the road! And sure enough, that was just when my mom came pulling up. I was terrified. Not only was this the second time, but Mom didn't make any pretense of calm this time. She was seething. She was red. And she kept a dull, dead silence. The calm, you know, before the storm. My butt wasn't the only thing bruised that day.

We got back to the home and my mother opened up. "What is it that you're thinking Irene?" She bashed me across the face with her open hand and I cringed. "What are you trying to do – ruin everything we work so hard for? Ruin our family? Is that what you're trying to do?" She grabbed me at the shoulders and shook me. "What am I supposed to make of it anymore? You … you …"

She lost any sense in her words after that as the screaming became more intense and the beating became more violent. She grabbed a flyswatter and began thrashing me all across my body until it broke. Then she beat me more with her hands until she just plain ran out of breath. I lay sobbing on the ground and Mom walked wearily off to her bedroom.

Dad wouldn't really wonder why dinner was late that night. And it wasn't hard for him to decipher me that night either. I was a mess of blood and scratches and bruises. I barely touched my food. My mom didn't look at me once. And I was seething like I never had in my little life. I was digging as fast I could, trying to bury and bury the raw, raw anger. But it kept seething. I would for months pointedly fear my mother. And I would, for months again, bury more and more of what I felt inside. So running away was not the answer. I would have to settle on avoiding, as much as I could and leaving for good as soon as I was old enough to go.

Chapter Nineteen

In the next year, things improved. Or, to put it another way, I stopped trying to run away, lived inside my bedroom, and more or less only dealt with verbal displeasure. The poor grades continued and more or less always would and Mom continued letting me know that it was a pointless venture to go to school each day. "By the time you're married and running a home, reading and writing are the only things you'll find useful. You learned those years ago." Never mind that I was only in fourth grade. "Dammit Irene …do you always have to remove so much potato with the skin? What do you think we'll have left to eat?" Helping around the home was as fruitless as Mom thought school was.

And of course worst of all was her constant harping on Margie. "What a girl!" my mom would say. "All smiles and nothing real about her. I know what she says about me behind my back, Irene. I know what you two talk about. Don't you believe a word that little snippet says, she lies about me so you will hate me. And look at you. *Look* at you. Always moping, always avoiding your mother – *your own mother*. And all because of one little girl's lies. Open your eyes, Irene. Open your eyes." It was weird, because when I did, all I could remember was Margie being kind to me and my mother beating me. And to tell the truth, Margie never bad-mouthed my mom. She just let me do so freely. Mom was certain that Margie had stolen my attention away from her, and I have to admit that it looked that way. But no human ever had room in her heart for just one person. I had room for many. Mom had pushed me away and Margie had done nothing but let me be her friend.

That fourth grade year a new threat arrived. A boy in first grade, but bigger than me, lived on a farm a little way past our home from the school. When he realized we were walking home the same way each day, he started following me and taunting me. I hated it, but I dealt with it. If living with my mom taught me something, it was how to live with being taunted.

But the taunting evolved and one day, I realized the taunting was coming closer and closer. When I turned, I saw that he was walking as fast as he could, cutting the distance between us. A panic surged through me. I hefted my bag up on my shoulder and began to run. He picked up his pace and closed the distance but I reached home before he caught me. I ran inside, breathless. "Now what is all this about?" asked my mother. "Running, holding those books? You trying to hurt yourself?"

"No Mom. Just for some exercise."

"You don't see me running places without reason do you?" she asked.

"No Mom. I'll try not to do it again." I hoped I didn't have to.

"Don't try. *Do*." Mom was a stickler on words when she wanted to be. "There's no poise in running. Remember to keep your poise."

"Yes Mom." I made off to my room. There was a reason I didn't tell her. A reason I hoped I never had to. I was already afraid of this boy. I was sure that her reaction would make me angry on top of scared.

The next day, this boy pulled the same stunt. And the next day. I only escaped the experience on the weekends. And although he never did catch me, I realized that was because he was letting me get away. Soon his taunts turned to telling me what would happen when he caught me – terrible things he said, most of which I didn't understand. But I knew it was terrible, because he was talking about pulling my clothes off and I knew how shameful that would be. It was hard to believe what I was hearing on my way home from school.

The fourth or fifth time I came home breathless, my mom chastised me again, and I was so frustrated, I accidentally told her. She furrowed her brow. "But he's just a little boy. You're going to tell me you let him chase you?" She shook her head slowly. "Irene, you know how I feel about your stories. You know how disappointed they make me. Don't bring some little boy into this just to cover yourself. I don't want you running, and that's final. You come in here like that again and you will go to bed without supper."

I did come in like that again. Many times. But Mom never sent me to bed without eating, and she never questioned me about it either. It was as if she really did believe me, but wanted nothing to do with it. So now, I was frightened, I was angry and I was desperate. School was bad enough. This made it a hundred times worse. And I had nowhere to turn until I confided in Margie.

Boy, that Margie. She wasn't afraid at all. She said she'd walk home with me, even though her house was in the other direction from school. And she did it. So there we were, two fourth grade girls and this bigger but younger boy starts taunting us from behind. All I can say is, thank God that the weather had turned cold. The pond at school had iced over and Margie had brought her ice skates to school for recess. Margie turned with her jaw set against this boy and taunted him right back. "Little boy think he's gonna do something to us? Come on little boy. Show us what you're gonna do."

That kid bolted right towards us. He was going to tackle the hell out of us and I could see demons in his eyes. Unbelievable that a six year old can look like that. But as he charged in, Margie grabbed her skates and swung them at him. *Bam!* That poor kid dropped and there was blood everywhere. She had caught him across the face.

Now, you think we were suddenly worried about whether he was okay? Think we were scared about what she'd done? Not a chance. Margie started screaming at him that he'd better leave me alone or she'd give him more of the same. Through his bawling, he must have heard her, because he ran home with his hands clasped over his face and never bothered me on my way home from school again.

○

That wasn't the last I saw of that boy. My parents were friendly with his, and wouldn't you know it, we were going to have to visit. It was around a year after the incident with the skates. Terror shook me, the way it did when I visited my cousins. I had already told my mom about this boy's taunting, had even told her that he threatened to pull my pants down, which had to be the ultimate embarrassment. Maybe that's why my mom disbelieved me, then never brought the subject up again. It was just like anything having to do with the differences between boys and girls. Never discussed.

I kept one hope and that was that my parents would let me stay with them during the visit. "Shh shh," said Mom when I asked. "You know that adult talk doesn't involve children. You kids go outside and play."

I didn't know what to do, but I was afraid. I ventured. I motioned that she come close for me to whisper. Mom listened in and I said, "I'm scared of him. He's not a nice boy at school. He says bad things about me."

Mom looked at me, then took me into the kitchen. "Irene, children sometimes do things to be mean at school because they don't know you. But then you have a chance to be friends with them and things change at school. Wouldn't you like that?" I shrugged. "Of course you would. Go make friends and play. And don't come back in while we're talking. You're a big girl now."

"But Mom …"

Mom stared hard. "Irene."

I ran outside. I didn't know where the kid was and I didn't know if what Mom said was true. I didn't really want to test her theory. Maybe if I could find a good place to hide, I could just curl up and spend the day unnoticed. Then when Mom asked whether I had fun, I could tell her that he wasn't a very nice boy but that I did okay. It would be the truth. Didn't matter if it was only a partial truth. Mom didn't ever need the whole truth so long as she was satisfied with what I said.

The family's farm was bordered by plenty of trees, so I headed out to the edge of their land and found my way in among the shade of leaves. There was a small clearing I could sit comfortably in, and I snuggled in against a sturdy tree. Now to wile away the hours. Maybe I could take a nap. Maybe I'd devise a way to skip out on these visits in the future. Maybe ….

A twig snapped and I looked up, startled. "Hi ugly baby." This kid was bad. I knew it. There wasn't any making friends.

"What do you want?" He had a scar across his face still from the skates.

"Where's your stinky friend and her skates? What, she isn't here? Too bad ugly baby. Now I have to pull down your pants like I said I would."

I wrapped my arms around my legs. "You wouldn't dare," I said. "It's not allowed. My parents will get you in so much trouble. Boys aren't supposed to see girls without their pants."

"Tough," he said, a very macho third grader. "Your parents aren't here and they won't know because if you tell them, I'll pull down your pants again in front of everyone at school."

"I'll scream. I'll scream and cry and your parents will take you away."

"They're all talking at the house, ugly baby. So shut up and take your pants off or I'll pull them off." I refused. I squeezed my arms around my legs as tightly as I could. But it didn't matter – that kid could wrestle trees. He pulled my arms apart in seconds and started yanking at my pants. I screamed and hit at him until he slapped me once across the face with brutal force. I was stunned. I stopped fighting. I clenched up and cried and cried, crawling deep inside myself. I don't know what all he did, but I know he took my clothes off and took his pants off, and that is all I remember. I wanted to be sick. I was utterly, utterly ashamed. There was no being a little kid after that, because a boy had seen me and I had seen him – had seen things I never should have at that time in my life. I didn't know what that meant, but I knew I was bad for letting him see. I knew I had been shamed. And I knew my mom would dismiss any story I told her.

I knew, but I tried. And I was right. She saw the bruise on my face the next day and asked what happened. I told her that the little boy attacked me and she said flatly, "Irene, he's a little boy. What could he do to you? And if you were attacked, we would have heard you out in the yard. I want you to stop passing the buck every time I ask you a question. Go to your room and think about that because I'm tired of telling you this lesson."

And boy oh boy was I tired of learning it.

Chapter Twenty

During the summer after sixth grade, reality became too real and the tale of Margie's aunt came back to haunt me. I thought from time to time about her outrageous stories about boys and girls and how things worked. But then, one summer afternoon, I went to use the outhouse and I quickly came running back in doors, scared that I was dying. "Mom," I screamed, "Mom help!"

My mom turned quickly and grabbed me around the shoulders. "Calm – calm! What is it Irene?"

"I'm bleeding," I said, starting to cry. "My pants ... just everywhere."

Mom's face became quite stern, but not towards me. It was as if she had to deal with some very foul business and she just had to make her way through to the end. "Quiet, Irene. It's ok. This is something that begins to happen when you're a young woman. I will get you something."

"Why is it happening though, Mom? Am I going to die?"

For once, on the topic of sex, I thought I almost saw my mom laugh. "No." She went to her bedroom and when she returned the veil of a great mystery lifted from over my head. Mom returned with a box. *The* box. The one she always got from old Mrs. Beckerman when she snuck to their door and knocked quietly at the Beckerman home. At last, I would understand that was all about.

Mom handed me the box. "Here, use these. You'll want to use them about once a month."

Once a month. That's when everything Margie's aunt had told us suddenly made sense. Now I knew what this was. Mom wouldn't say another word on the subject, but now the situation was clear and I knew what I had to do. Thank God for Margie's aunt. I could believe my mom, now, that I wouldn't die. But I wished that Mom had told me herself. From what I was learning about life, there was supposed to be a kind of bond between a mother and daughter and that secrets like this would be opened up between them. For me, that bond did not exist. And as much as my mom seemed to want that bond when she harassed Margie for taking me away, for example, these moments came and went when the bond was meant to be formed. And it never was.

○

After avoiding the topic itself, however, Mom did seem to want to make something of this event. It seemed that she would go after some of that bonding and I wanted to see where this went. "You know, Irene, you've obviously a young woman now. I think we can celebrate a little by going to town (this meant the larger town where I was born) and getting you something nice to wear – something fit for a young lady."

I could hardly believe my ears. Mom still made my clothes by hand. Funds were a little better these days, but since dresses were easy enough to make, Mom didn't feel that squandering extra money on dresses made any sense. Better to save, or to enjoy those things we couldn't make at home.

I put on my nicest dress with two ideas in mind. First, I wanted to feel good about myself as we went to shop. Second, I wanted Mom comparing the new dress to an old one, the best of the old ones, so that whatever I got was actually a good deal. On a warm afternoon with eighth grade approaching, the three of us went to town. We would get the new dress, along with any other clothes Mom thought I needed for my venture into the next grade. As we approached a store, I saw some girls walking by in jeans, and I thought … just maybe. Maybe, since I had reached a definitely new stage, going into eighth grade, I could have some jeans to wear. I wasn't a little girl anymore. Mom had to know that. Though the little girls didn't wear jeans to school, many older ones did. I wanted to be more like the rest of the kids and maybe make a break from the way things had always been in the early grades. Maybe kids had grown up enough by now that, if I were a little more like them, they would accept me.

"Mom?" I asked.

"Yes Irene." Mom walked so straight, she was a poster-woman for good posture. The way a lady should walk, she often told me and I never did argue that one.

"Since I'm going into eighth grade, could I get some clothes a little like the other girls? I mean, see those girls there? They've got on jeans and they look so nice, don't you think?"

Mom stopped, but stood as erect as when she walked. She looked at me, disappointed. "Those girls? *Those girls?* Irene, what is it with you wanting everything that is wrong with this world? The *zoot suiters* – those awful girls. Is that who you want to be like? Girls wearing jeans and hating the world? You want to spend your life hating the world and rebelling?"

"Not the *girls*, Mom. The *jeans*. I don't want to hate the world."

"The kind of girls that wear jeans are the kind that hate the world, Irene. You don't need to be in with crowds like that. And besides, Irene, you need a flat stomach to wear jeans. Those girls have flat stomachs, see? Your stomach sticks out." She poked me in my gut. "You would look awful in jeans. Trust your mother. We'll get you a nice dress and a few blouses and we'll keep you looking as nice as you can."

As nice as you can. Good God! I wondered if she heard the words coming out. But she didn't show any remorse about the comments, so I wondered whether it was intentional torture or just oblivion. In either case, I was crushed that my mom could say something so hurtful about my appearance and once again, I found myself digging deeper inside. I would hardly utter a word. I would nod my head when my mom showed me what she chose for me to wear and I focused on holding back the tears.

Not a flat enough stomach to look good. Ok, I would remember that one. It was the match that was going to light the fuse at last. I vowed that day that my explosion would rock our little town.

Chapter Twenty-One

There are exceptions to everything, but if any parent wants to know, there's plenty of research about how to keep a kid from tick-tick-ticking and then one day going off. I know, half the time it's a shock to everyone that a kid is doing drugs or committing crimes or joining a gang or anything else. Sometimes, no doubt about it, the parents have done everything right under their own roof, and if they hold fault at all, it is because they didn't stretch their dominion out a little further to know what influences were going on at school, during sports, or whatever. But the whole dominion thing is a mighty trick. Where do you draw the line? There's never a clear answer and never an exact one. That's part of what makes parenting a challenge. So a parent's fault in this way is really pretty minimal if they have done their best to strike a balance between dominion and allowing freedoms.

But plenty of kid-explosions out there could be predicted by any psych student in the world. First, the explosion is fueled by things repressed. I don't mean by memories so repressed that someone can't remember them. It doesn't have to be so severe. But if someone has to bury themselves over and over again through life, never venting anger, frustration, feelings in general, you've got fuel for a bomb that you never want to see go off.

That's part one. A fueled bomb might not ever go off. You need something to set the explosion, and that comes from the whole dominion versus freedom thing. There has to be a balance, because too far to either side, you've got yourself some trouble. Parents wanting to give their kids all the slack in the world are going to find that slack taken and they're going to be surprised by how badly they mess up their kids lives. I don't understand, they too often say. I let him do everything he wanted, and he still got into so much trouble. Give 100 kids free run of a candy store and just see how many of them end up sick. It's supposed to be basic knowledge, the whole boundary thing, but it's still a shock to some. Without boundaries, you're not repressing the child but you're bound to be putting out fires so long as they're under your care, only because you're letting the child light them.

Alternately, you've got the parents who figure that, through complete control of their children, they can decide every outcome. It's the old debate of whether it is better to have people love you or to have a people fear you. Same with kids. If you try to control every outcome, you're bound to promote repression after repression which fuels the bomb. If you work this control to just the right degree, you might only add the fuel. If you go too far, you're bound to strike the match that sets the whole thing off.

As I've said before, if you put my mom beside some parents, she looks good. We've all heard stories that chill us and, if we are zealous for the safety of children, that boil us at the same time. But again, the whole point is that she was the kind of mother that is far too common – someone who feels she must dominate. It's a plague on our children when we raise them in such a desperate way. Like so many, Mom played the control game far too hard and crafted herself a homemade bomb, the way parents do who will never end up as the headline mothers who drowns their children. Instead, their kids end up in the headlines.

In Mom's case, the process was as steady as wash, rinse, repeat, but was less healthy than keeping things clean. It went like this – make decisions for your girl, speak for her, do everything for her, beat her when you must, and compare her to an elusive perfect child and let her know that she is falling short. Repeat. Continue until you have lit a fateful match.

When my mom made that one little comment about how I would look in jeans, I became committed to getting even. In fact, I would make the whole town pay for the way most of the kids had rejected me. Only Margie and a handful of others had become friends in all these years. They would be spared. In fact, as I started to make my plans, I decided that they would help me take my vengeance.

The flat-stomach comment got me back into my bedroom. I didn't want to see my mom anymore. I was sick of feeling stupid, ugly, unwanted. The rebellion began and before long, I would be the *zoot suiter* that women talked about. Into eighth grade, Margie and I took up the trademark habit of *zoot suiterrs* everywhere. We began to smoke.

All my years growing up, I had a great distaste for smoking. My father smoked. I remember him sitting with a can of tobacco and a package of papers, rolling his cigarettes. I also remember a permanent yellow stain on his two left fingers. He was right handed, so the way I figured it, he spent the day using his right hand for work and his left hand for smoking. What an ugly tattoo, forever to be marked by cigarettes like that! Smoking never appealed to me.

Sure, as a little kid, it was fun to pretend I was smoking with my friends. I mean, we would get those candy cigarettes, white sugar with a bit of red at one end. Mom wouldn't let me buy them, but I'd get them from kids at school and we'd sit around pretending we were grown up. The appeal was pretending to be grown up. When I let my imagination wander into future years, all I could see was freedom from home and parents and that made candy cigarettes a fun sort of escape.

But then we hit eighth grade. That poor teacher. She was arthritic and generally ill, and she couldn't handle her students. We were basically given books and assignments and would have to tackle it all on our own. Her presence was honestly just a technicality.

At first, we would just wander across the street into the woods during recess and lunch breaks, and there, we'd roll our own cigarettes. Mind you, these weren't what you'd call premium cigarettes. No, we'd roll them in pieces of paper torn from brown paper bags and what we actually smoked was any dried leaves or twigs we could find. Yeah, they were that gross. But it felt good, like a big middle finger that I could wag at my parents every time I smoked.

We kept that up until Margie found a way to bring real cigarettes to school. I even helped the cause once in a while. If Dad bought a pack of formed cigarettes, I would steal one from the pack without his knowing. Guess I didn't include that in my earlier stealing disclosure. This was at least one more example.

Anyway, with real cigarettes to look forward to, Margie and I made smoking a more frequent habit than just recesses and lunch. One of us would excuse ourselves to the outhouse and we'd light up out there, take a few puffs, then return to class. The other would then head outdoors, take a few more puffs, then return. We usually didn't stop with one trip each. We'd keep taking turns heading outside until the cigarette was gone or we'd just had enough. The poor teacher never said a word about us leaving so much. I guess she knew she couldn't do a thing about it anyway.

That was the early stage of my rebellion. I had committed to making my parents and the community suffer for everything I'd gone through as a child and that commitment was still on. After any number of my mother's snubbing during eighth grade, I'd finally had it and during retreats to my room, I started developing a very specific plan – a plan that would wreak havoc on our little town of thirty five people, a town whose suburb population may have brought us up to an incredible 100 residents. If the population was small, I would not be. I would be the most well-known, the most feared person in town. And my posse would help me rule.

Or, that's how I envisioned it.

To my discredit, I didn't do much research to anticipate support. To my credit, I was a little young for this kind of research.

The thing developed because I was a second child without a sibling to look to for example, without a parent to look to for example either, because Mom was my clear and present enemy, and Dad was around for meals and bedtime and that was about it. He wasn't any protection from the enemy, so he was, in this scenario, in the bad camp. That meant, what was bad for them was good for me.

Mom's mistake was to point out so distinctly the worst role model possible – the *zoot suiters*. The bad girls. The girls who wore what I couldn't wear, who did what I couldn't do, who lived a risky life. The worse she made them out to be, the more they became my role models. But they weren't quite bad enough, because their general attitude didn't make them stand out, as I was determined to do.

So the scheme developed, crafted in my mind by a thousand resentments, by a mother who shrugged off my education, who harassed me about not helping out around the home and who dwelt on the fact that I would never open up, even while she continued to shut me down.

Truth was, she wouldn't much like what she saw if I opened up anyway. She would see the plan and it is terrible in its potential. She would see a big city criminal wrapped up inside this small town girl. And she would know that it was her fault.

She would see it all soon enough, for I was dead set on action. I would start a gang. Not just any gang, but one that would hold an entire community captive. That's right. We would wear jeans and leather jackets, just the clothes my mom would never allow. We would meet at night to work our terrors. The clearest idea of all was that we would trespass throughout the town, grab sleeping dogs by their hind legs, and with the devil's pleasure, we would swing the little mutts in a circle and launch them through the air.

My little brain didn't get so far as to picture what would happen next. We would be a terror. The town would wonder whether Judgment Day was upon them, and I would be the rider on the pale horse.

Or something like that. I wasn't well enough studied in Biblical terms to think of it in that way. But if I were so well studied, that's just how bad I was sure my gang would be.

I was crafty about it all. I picked out a clubhouse location. No one knew what I was up to. I selected my gang members. Not one person had a clue. And so, with this death knell for the town worked out, I approached Margie and with careful precision, sketched it all for her to see.

That is where my lack of research brought it all crashing down.

"Why would we want to do all of that?" asked Margie.

"To get back at them. The kids have never liked me here and my mom has insulted me as long as I can remember. This town needs a wake-up call."

Margie shrugged. "I don't know. My parents are pretty cool. I don't think they need a wake-up call. And kids are kids. Who cares if they want to play in their own little circles? I've got you as a friend. They've got themselves.

And you can't make the parents or their dogs pay for kids not wanting to play with us." She paused and looked at me quizzically. "Dogs, Irene? Really?"

"Well, people love their dogs. It would teach them a thing or two."

Margie looked doubtful. "Like I said, the dogs didn't do anything. And if we got caught, my parents would be so angry. I'd lose a bunch of privileges."

"I don't have any," I pointed out.

"Well I do. I don't want to upset my parents. I don't want to lose the privilege of hanging out with you. And your mom would probably be so mad that I'd never see you again. Think about that."

In the end, Margie was the good-child influence on me. In a few minutes, she diffused the whole idea of a gang – all the planning, all the anticipation of real vengeance. It just melted away, leaving me with the age-old pain of feeling that my mother cared so little, that she threatened so much, and that I still wanted to get out just as soon as I could.

Chapter Twenty-Two

As I pushed on into my teenage years, I discovered a new kind of challenge to having an overprotective mother and an under-interested dad. I started the change from little girl to young woman, and with the change came a desire for more social interaction and – boys.

Our small town didn't supply many options. Few of the boys were my age, and none of the kids had ever let me into their groups. But Margie was my way out. Her parents demanded responsibility of her and in return, she earned privileges reasonable for her age. They had always been good about taking us out into a larger town where every person didn't know every other, where there were actually stores to choose from where there was variety and what I always felt was excitement.

Mom would let me go with them because, after getting to know them, she felt that they were as protective and controlling as she was. Their demand for responsibility gave that impression, and Mom had never seen the privileges that went with the demands. She was sure we would always be watched on our excursions. Well, we were for a time – when we were young enough that it was important. But as we got older, they gave us freedom and by the time we reached fifteen, they let us stay in town to go to parties with other kids. We just had to get home before it was too late. Even at that age, Mom wouldn't let me sleep at Margie's because she thought it invited trouble. She let me stay out till 10:30 on weekends, and that was enough for time at parties. Of course she would have flipped if she knew what was going on and that would have been the end of my Margie days so long as I was under her roof. But that was the beauty of our adventures being in another town.

During the spring when I was sixteen, Margie and I went on a town excursion with her parents. We were browsing through a clothing store as we often did Margie sometimes got to buy a shirt or pants for school, and I just loved the chance of feeling so many fabrics and imagining myself in something fresh, new and store-bought. The store was four times the size of Beckermans, but didn't deal with all of life's essentials. No, it had clothes, aisles and aisles of clothes and I loved to get lost amidst them.

As I was sorting through jeans with just a shred of guilt, I heard a couple girls nearby talking about a party, and when I looked up I recognized them from a party we'd been to a few months before. I smiled. "Hi guys."

One of the girls looked more or less indifferent, but the other smiled. "Hi. Haven't seen you around for a while. It's Amy, isn't it?"

"Irene," I said. "You guys are lucky to have so much going on around here."

"That's right," said the indifferent girl, "you're from out in the sticks, aren't you? Gotta be so dull there. Well, it's not much better here. We just all try to hang out so we're not too bored."

"Well, you've got people to hang out with. We've got all of a hundred people living anywhere near us and most aren't our age."

"Hey, you're welcome to hang out here," said the indifferent girl. Only she wasn't so indifferent now. She saw that I was basically like them.

I shrugged my shoulders. "We don't get out here too often. Wish we could."

"Well come on to the party tonight then," said the first girl, "might as well see people while you can."

I smiled. "We'd love to. I mean … It's ok if Margie comes?" I gestured with my thumb over my shoulder to show who I meant. The girls nodded and that was our ticket in for the night.

Margie's parents dropped us off later that evening and before they left, we arranged for rides home. It was a generic arrangement. Everyone at the party said that someone would drop us off, so we let her parents take off.

It was very typical for a teenage party. The guys were doing and saying things to monopolize attention and the girls pretended to be impressed. I was guilty of a little of that myself. Kids were drinking. A couple guys wrestled out in the backyard, like rams proving their prowess to their potential mates. A couple of the girls flirted heavily with the hottest guys until they coaxed them off into bedrooms and you wouldn't see them for another half an hour. After a while, the other guys started feeling left out. They started looking around for their own prey so they could come over and breathe alcohol in our faces, telling us about whatever exploits they thought would adequately impress the girls into action.

For my own part, I may have had as much as a beer, though that much would have been a stretch. I hated alcohol on a number of levels, and I while one beer would probably be good for most teenagers, it would have been more than enough for me because I was wound up to explode. Were I not repulsed by alcohol, I could see myself getting lost in it. In the first place, alcoholism ran in my family. My dad might have let it run his own life, except he had my mom to do that instead and she kept him from becoming a drunk. But she couldn't keep the extended family from that. Still, we weren't allowed to call anyone an alcoholic. Instead, they were drunks. There was an enormous stigma surrounding the word "alcoholic," but there wasn't much of an issue around drunks. Extraordinary.

My grandfather – also a *drunk* – made moonshine in the woods behind his home. Everyone in the community knew he made it, but no one said a word because it was illegal. But there was a day when I was staying at my grandparents' home. I was about seven years old. Curious as heck about where my grandfather was going, I headed out into the woods to see him. I came to a small clearing where he sat with a bottle in one hand. I watched quietly for a long time while he drank. Finally, though, I decided I'd go and say hello. It didn't matter to me that he was drinking. A hello couldn't hurt.

Boy was I wrong. The minute I stepped into sight, this horrid shadow crossed his face. He became what I imagined evil spirits look like – contorted, grotesque and angry. He stood, then staggered and I ran. But I was in such a panic, I tripped over a log while looking for the path. Grandpa caught me and started slapping the hell out of me. I was stinging all over until I either blacked out or just repressed everything that happened. All I remember is the beating, and then loathing him ever since. Add all that to the fact that – hey, let's admit it – beer just tastes *awful* so it's no wonder I laid off the stuff. I drank just enough to fit in. And fitting in was what I was doing at the party that night when I became a target.

A guy named Jim found prey for his own drunken flirtation. He was telling me about how he'd be a starting pitcher for the high school baseball team that year. I started getting sick from his breath. It wasn't fun. It wasn't pretty. I saw another guy pull Margie off toward the opposite end of the room to corner her and talk her ear off, so I was basically on my own and getting desperate. If I was interested in guys, I wasn't interested in *this* guy. And definitely not when he was drunk. With only a few sips of beer in me, I was one of the few sober people at the party and I was all too familiar with how ridiculous the kids looked, smelled and sounded when they were drunk. Jim had a nice buzz and a terrible stink about him. I spent a while trying to hold my breath while nodding about his heroic baseball feats.

"Oh, you don't say – three strike outs in one inning? That's something." Deep breath.

Many nods. Conclusion of another speech. "Oh, two doubles in one game? Good for you!" Deep breath. Many nods. And so on.

I watched the clock on the wall behind him carefully, and as the hands crept towards 10:00 I felt him inching inwards for a bit of contact. I finally told him, "Well Jim, you sure are a great baseball player. But you know what? I've got to be home by 10:30 so I've got to find a ride home."

He blinked. "I'll give you a ride," he said. "Sure, no problem. I can drive you home."

"What about Margie?"

"Oh, she can come too. Sure, why not?" His words were a little slurred, but I thought that it was either part show or he was a real light weight. He'd probably had a couple beers total. I hoped it was a show. There wouldn't be many other drivers on the road home, but there were plenty of trees lining the roads and I didn't want to end the night in a drunken wreck.

"Wait here," I told him. "I'll go find Margie."

Margie was glad for the rescue. "Oh, sorry Scott," she was saying. "I guess we're heading home. Um … it's been nice …." She didn't bother finishing the sentence. He was in a daze. We both wondered if he knew she was leaving.

"Margie," I whispered, "do you have anyone who can take us home?"

She looked at me. "No. I thought you were getting me because you found someone."

I shook my head. "I've got this guy who'll take us home but I don't want him to. I was hoping there was someone better."

Margie laughed quietly, keeping it between us. "I don't know anyone here either. How many options do you think we have?" She laughed again as we both looked around at guys proving their bravado, girls pretending to like it and the group as a whole getting a little more drunk with every passing minute. We giggled together. "Might as well take what we can get, otherwise you're going to be late getting home." I agreed and reluctantly went to get Jim.

We made it out to the car and our chauffeur pulled back into the street, then hit the gas to send dirt flying out behind us. "Yeah, this bad boy's got some power," Jim told us. "I know this guy down at the garage …." He went into the details about how he was able to soup up the car so that he could beat just about any other kid's car. He went on about a bunch more things too. Margie and I both zoned out, and before we knew it, we were pulling into our little town, or hamlet by comparison. We soon dropped Margie off.

"Ok, where to Irene?" I told him how to get to my house. It was just a couple minutes after 10:30. That would be ok with my parents. But down the road from the house, we stopped. "Hang on just a second," he told me. He shut off the car and hopped out. *Too much beer. He's gotta go,* I figured. But then, my own door opened and Jim was there. He looked at me just a second, then was in the car on top of me.

I flashed back many years to the bully from school who had molested me out in the woods near his home and a violence erupted in me. I screamed out loud – *loud!* I screamed and screamed. I kicked at him and punched him. But he was too strong for me to stop and probably too drunk to feel my punches. Despite my flying fists, he got most of my blouse undone and had pushed my skirt up. But his own pants proved too complex. He had to use two hands to get them down and it gave me a chance to bring my knee up. *Hard.* Drunk or not, he felt that and crumpled onto the car floor. I slipped from the car, turned once more to scream at him, then fled to my house, buttoning up my shirt as fast as I could.

When I got inside, Mom just looked at me and looked at the clock. It was 10:40. She could see that I was breathless. "A little better effort to make it by 10:30 next time, please," she said. I didn't tell her what happened. I wanted there to be a next time. Only, I'd get out at Margie's house and walk home.

O

A week into that summer, Margie and I were planning to hit another party in a different town. Mom didn't know about the party, but she knew Margie's parents were taking us out of town for the evening. As I said goodbye and headed out the door, Mom looked at me and said, "Please Irene, no screaming out on the road tonight. A little courtesy for people who are trying to sleep."

I nodded curtly so Margie wouldn't see and got outside as fast as I could. "What's that about?" asked Margie.

"I don't know," I told her. "Maybe someone was making a racket before I got home." But that moment said more than anything up to that time in my life. Mom had heard me screaming. Mom hadn't done a thing about it. Why? I didn't know and I don't now. But I was 16 at that time and I vowed to get out from beneath her roof within a year.

Chapter Twenty-Three

I was sixteen, and Mom seemed to be dealing with two sides of herself. One side was sick to death of fighting with me. A good daughter wasn't supposed to fight. She was supposed to listen to her mother, do as her mother did, then marry and continue on the tradition. Where did this girl get the notion that she could talk back and be angry at her mother? It was school, that Margie girl and these damn modern ways of thinking. They were all to blame. And after sixteen years, she was just tired of fighting it every step of the way. The other side of her loved to battle and could never wait for our next round.

This inner clash meant that I got out from under her roof a surprising number of times, considering how much control she still wished to hold over me. But then when I came back and the words began, escalating always into screams and sometimes more. Often these battles were based on whatever I had been allowed to go and do, to the point that I sometimes wondered why I didn't just stay home instead until I was old enough to live on my own.

Summer arrived and Margie had one of her great ideas. We would go camping at a nearby lake. Her aunt would chaperone. And it wasn't just Margie and me. We invited a couple of Margie's cousins and one of my own to come along. There would be gaggle of us ladies. I couldn't wait. Although I hated bugs, they were generally a lesser nuisance than my mother's snapping.

We hung out at the beach, had roaring fires at night and shared girl talk all weekend. Margie's aunt was a great story teller and kept us laughing all the time. And there was freedom, the blessed freedom that I knew wasn't far off every day of my life. It felt good, as it always did to be out with Margie and to be myself.

The camping went without incident that year. We had so much fun that, the next year, we decided to do it again. Only this time, things were a little different, as they always are when you try to repeat something great. Don't get me wrong, the second camping trip was a blast. More fun, really, than the first year had been. But it ended up getting me back into hot water with my mom, which by this point was of course no surprise, yet no less hell to endure.

This second year was enormously different, even though the same group headed out together. We began our few days with girl talk, had a nice campfire and sleepover together. Next day, though, we headed into a nearby town and Margie and I met a few other girls and some guys. Not much need to say, that shifted the value of girl talk in our minds. Our cousins were a few years younger than we were, so hanging out with a group our age was very appealing. They were camping not far from us so that evening we went to spend time with them.

The girls and guys in the group all had not chosen partners. No danger in a little flirting, something I saw little point in doing even in my high school, where there were too many losers. As my mom had so delicately pointed out during the jeans event and so often afterwards I had a few extra pounds that kept me from feeling as beautiful as I wanted to. But in a situation like this, we were welcomed into the group for a visit, and that gave us a couple days with them. It was a relaxed atmosphere, and I was immediately liked just for being me. So I was at ease and didn't hesitate to have some fun with flirting.

The group was planning to stay for several more days. There was no way to call home and change plans because our parents didn't have a phone. So when Margie's aunt went to take our cousins home, we sent them with a message. We would have our parents pick us up three days later.

There was a reason besides the guys that made me really want to stay. My parents had sold their home in order to build a new one in a neighboring town. The new house would be a step up, but until we moved in we faced a mighty step down. We had to move back into the two-room home where I grew up. This time, I had the bedroom to myself and my parents slept in the common room. But we were again without electricity and of course still without any plumbing. It was cramped quarters with strange and haunting memories of a childhood where I was absolutely bound to my mother's aura. Floods of thoughts came back about the earliest snips and snaps my mother made about everything I did and didn't do. It was uncomfortable. And it was the most boring place on earth with literally nothing to do but think my thoughts and wander the dirt paths across the farm.

So camping, and especially camping with guys, was heaven-sent. As during the first year, nothing really extraordinary happened during the trip. I simply and happily had a time to enjoy and later remember fondly. But then, my parents came to pick me up.

Apparently, they were none too pleased about the change in plans without their say-so. Apparently, too, they didn't mind the extra time alone because they had not objected to our change of plans. But when they saw our campground, when they saw the guys with us it was all over. No beating this time. But the silent treatment. In a lot of ways, that was a good thing. I wouldn't have to listen to my mother for some time. But in one important way, it was very bad. If I had felt unloved by my parents all my life, that feeling was magnified tenfold during the silent treatment, which had increasingly been her tactic after I outgrew my mom's real ability to beat me.

On the car ride home, Mom said not a word. That day, that night, and the next week she said not a word. I dealt with it well for many days. It started getting itchy by the end of a week. I was feeling desperate and lonely. Why do we suppose so many kids rebel? Because they are looking for attention, any kind of attention, from those who are meant to love them. We often interpret attention as love, no matter what kind of attention it is. So despite all my mother's awful words about me, over time they were better than no words at all.

As depression settled in, my few extra pounds became a few more. I ate because it was a way to console myself. As I consoled myself, I gained some pounds. And eventually those pounds ended the silence. It was maybe three weeks after we came home that Mom spoke to me, "Irene, what is this? You're putting on weight? God *damn* you girl! It's just as I thought. Camping out there with boys like that. Look at you now, a God damned pregnant teenager. Have I taught you nothing in all these years? Did I teach you to sleep around? Well, young lady, don't think I'm here to raise your child. You'll drop out of school now, because you're looking after that baby yourself. Christ above —"

"But Mom, I didn't sleep with anyone."

Mom stood from the table and looked at me hard. Then without warning, she reached out and grabbed my stomach and shook what she could grab. "You look at this and tell me you're not pregnant. Sleeping around like some tramp. What *will* people think about how I've raised you?"

I blushed a deep red. I was nervous, ashamed, and angry all at once. "But Mom, I'm *not* sleeping around. I've never been with a boy and I don't want to be. There just hasn't been much to do here this summer. I've probably eaten too much."

"Oh, *I* see. Now it's Mom's and Dad's fault for moving you to the country. Don't you try turning your blame around on us. I swear to you, Irene, you are in for a heap of trouble. Spent your whole life turning blame around on people. Well you watch out for the real world. People aren't going to put up with that. They're all going to turn you out on your ear."

"I didn't *say* it was your fault, Mamma. I'm not pregnant, and it's not your fault that I'm bored. I'm just bored. That's all!" Both our voices were on the rise. It was ridiculous that so much could come out of one impossible deduction. After all if I were three weeks pregnant, I wouldn't be showing at all. But I didn't know that then and it wasn't an issue to my mom.

"Well don't you worry about being bored any more. We've got a trip to fill some of your time tomorrow. We're going to the doctor and he'll straighten all this out. We'll have proof once and for all that you're a terrible liar. Then maybe you'll respect me just a little when I tell how things are. I wasn't born just yesterday, but you're a damned teenager and you never want to admit it."

Tears were streaming down my face. I hurried to my bedroom. I couldn't believe I would have to visit the doctor about a pregnancy that, as far as I knew, was an impossibility. I cried myself to an early sleep that night.

I was saved the next day by my period. When I showed my mom that I was having it she nodded curtly and walked away. She let another two days go by before she spoke with me again. Those two days were good for me. They let me think on everything that had happened and I started reflecting on one thing in particular. She had said I'd have to drop out of school to take care of the baby. I was already through with eleventh grade. Considering my small-town, non-academic future, maybe leaving school wasn't such a bad idea. It could get me out of my home. I would think on it. For now, I would venture into twelfth grade and just see how it all worked out.

Chapter Twenty-Four

When it finally comes time, you look back. You appreciate the way time and events led to the present moment and the present you. You appreciate how some of the roughest qualities of others have helped make you who you are and despite whatever flaws you have, no matter how much you wish to still improve, you wouldn't change who you've become.

At age seventeen, though, that time hadn't yet come. The harsh reality of my mother was still too fresh and I wasn't looking back. I wanted to know only three things. How could I get out? When could I get out? And how could I make sure I never went back again?

What is amazing to me now is that my mom had often struck the match that should have set off my own personal explosion. I had so much repressed that I know I was set to go off. But when I wanted to start a gang, Margie was there to diffuse me. There were times after that when Margie's damned first-child personality kept me balanced, because she wanted to please, to live up to expectations, to be responsible. So all the repression stayed where it was and would have to surface at a later time. I didn't know how or when.

As I entered my senior year of high school, school was the same ol' same ol'. I was learning things, but to me, influenced by my parents' perspective, the work I did to learn was essentially wasted work. I was learning things I would never use, because as much as I hated the notion, I would marry someone local though hopefully not as local as my parents always said, because there was really no appealing choice in my home town. I would probably end up on a farm. And though I had never learned to do domestic chores mother's way, I would figure it out. I would run a household and bear children, so reading, writing, and arithmetic would truly be the extent of the knowledge I used.

With all this in mind and as angry as I still was at my mother, it was easy to be tempted, and tempted I was. My cousin had escaped his own house of chaos a year earlier by getting himself a job. Now it was my turn. I skipped out on a class and went to a nearby store to make a phone call. "Johnny, it's me," I said when my cousin answered. "I need to get out. I need to get a job."

I could practically hear him grinning over the phone. "Good for you!" he said. "Listen, the creamery where I'm working, they've got an opening for a receptionist. Give 'em a call." Soon as we hung up, I called and arranged an interview. The manager agreed to see me the next day and I was offered a job on the spot.

I headed back to school to see my homeroom teacher. "Mr. Gunner, I just wanted to let you know that I won't be seeing you any more. I've got a job and I'll be dropping out of school."

Mr. Gunner was a good man and sincere. We weren't that close or anything, but I thought he should know. He didn't want to let me off so easily though. He looked at me carefully. "Irene, why are you dropping out?"

"Because I got a job," I repeated.

"No, Irene. I mean, why are you getting a job before you're done with school? Don't you know how much a high school degree will do for you?"

"It doesn't do as much for me as a job," I explained. "If I get a job, I get out on my own and can do what I want."

"It might look that way right now, Irene. But without graduating, you won't have as much freedom as you will after graduation. A high school degree will open a lot of doors for you that will never open without it. Think about it Irene. You've come so far. You have less than a year to go. If you really want to be free, if you really want to do whatever catches your interest, graduation is the key."

I shrugged my shoulders. "Maybe, Mr. Gunner. But it doesn't do anything for me now and it doesn't do me much good if I spend the rest of my life on a farm."

"Who says you're going to?" he asked me. "Who says you have to live all your life on a farm. Do you know how many jobs there are in the cities? The future is in the cities, Irene. Without an education, you don't have the tools for that future."

I shrugged again. "Don't see how I'll ever end up in the cities when I live all the way out here."

"It can happen in a day," he told me. "We never know what's going to happen tomorrow, and we sure don't know how. Think about it Irene. Promise me you'll at least think about what you're giving up."

"Ok," I told him. But I doubt I ever gave it a second thought. I had only one motivation at that time, a motivation that had built in me all my life. And that was to get away from home.

Luckily, Mom and Dad didn't care one way or another. They were literally without emotion on the subject. I told them and my dad just looked at me and said, "Ok, we'll help you find a place to stay." And that was that. I should have been suspicious, but I wasn't. Stupid, stupid, stupid.

Before long I was in a one-room apartment in the basement of a home. It shared a bathroom with other one-room apartments and it was within walking distance of work. And most important of all it was not my parents' home.

I was out. I was free at last. The only question for me now was, what would the future hold?

Life is full of ironies, so it's no surprise that the answer was ironic. The future, with all its promised freedom, was chock full of more control.

Now, the wise reader will nod and say, "Yes, of course. Everyone imagines that getting away from the parents will lead into this blissful freedom, but they don't realize how much responsibility there is to living on your own. Your freedom would be hindered by all those hours of work. You'd have to give most of your money away to bills and so on. So the freedom you think you'll win is really just an illusion." And that wise reader would of course be accurate in many respects. But that is not the kind of control I'm talking about. Despite the work and the bills, I did still feel free. Problem was, regardless of where I lived, Mom wasn't quite ready to let go of my life.

If I had to spend all week working, that was fine if I had the weekends to myself. But I didn't. Mom and Dad insisted on driving into my new hometown and picking me up for the weekend; if I had other plans, they went just about ballistic. I was still their little girl. They were still my parents. And I shouldn't ever forget what they had done for me. I should still want to be with them when time allowed. Was I already such a city girl that I was embarrassed to remember my roots? And there I was, wondering if my mom ever knew, all the years I had buried myself in my room, that I never wanted to be with her because I was afraid of her and angry with her. Time with her only proved one thing – I could never be the daughter she wanted me to be. So who would want to spend time dwelling on that?

For all their fits, I still did want and need to enjoy some of my freedom, and for a year or two on my own, I made friends, went to some parties and finally, dated some guys. But the magic never happened. I wondered if there was such thing as magic. The life experience I had was full of arguments or isolation. Perhaps that's all that marriage was. Perhaps I was really just to raise children on my own, and that was life.

But one night, during an evening dinner with the family I ended up rooming and boarding with, I received a phone call. Nothing unusual in that, until I picked up the phone and found myself talking with the most popular boy from high school, Bob. I almost dropped the phone when I heard him introduce himself. Why was *he* calling *me*? He didn't remember me from school, no one really did. But he had seen me at the creamery where I was working and now was calling to ask me for a date.

If there was any punctuation mark to my experience with my mother, if there was a time that showed most clearly what she really was to me, it was the time that followed this phone call. It's not that my parents were against me getting married, but I think they always believed they would decide who and when. In fact, my parents had already chosen a farmer living near them for me to marry. But from the beginning, my heart was with Bob and his was with me.

Chapter Twenty-Five

Bob should have been everything they hoped for because, no matter how much I hated seeing my parents anymore, he insisted we visit them on Sundays. I never resented Bob for that. I was too in love, and he insisted because he wanted to do the right thing. No question, I was in love with a good guy. But every Sunday, those conversations with my parents were strained. Every Sunday, Mom tried to tell us what to do and how to do it. This was an eye-opener, a new experience, for Bob. But he wouldn't back down. He felt that parents were an important part of someone's life. I couldn't deny that, but for me, important could be a positive or negative term. Secretly, Mom and Dad were disappointed that I wasn't dating their chosen farmer. The whole time Bob and I dated, they hoped he would some day disappear and I would see the wisdom of the choice that they had made so long ago. Well, I hated to disappoint them, but Bob was it. After a couple years of dating, we became engaged. I spoke with Mom in private one day to tell her.

How crestfallen she was! What a look of disappointment spread across her face! "Irene, I can't pretend I'm happy to hear this. You know, it's really better if you can marry a farmer nearby, because otherwise what will happen to this land we've put so much of our soul into? You think it's going to farm itself? No. It needs a man. And your Bob is no farmer."

I creased my brow and shook my head. "Mother ... I've been dating Bob for two years and we are completely in love. Do you really think I'm going to just drop him for some land?"

"Irene, don't you talk that way about this farm! Your entire life springs from this farm. Don't ever forget your roots." She frowned. "But I know. I know you will stay with Bob. So we will put on the wedding for you, if you'll just bring Bob over to discuss the plans. Don't tell your father. I'll let him down gently before you come to talk about the wedding."

Let him down gently. Great. He still thought I would be married to the land and their farmer boy? For all I cared, that farmer could be a great guy or a scoundrel. That wasn't the point. I just didn't get their bizarre hopes for me to lose Bob.

We visited my parents on the following Sunday to discuss wedding plans. Was I in for a surprise! We sat down, very excited because we had a number of things in mind. And then Mom spoke.

"Great news, Irene. You can get married in June, right after the seeding is finished. Here's the guest list, all the important people included. We'll book the hall and have the Maduski family cater. You can make the decorations. So what we really need is for you to pick out a dress and let us know who your bridesmaids will be. Oh, it'll be beautiful. Your wedding will be so beautiful.

"Oh, and Bob, the guest list is already very long. You understand. There are so many people that have to come, because we've been invited to their sons' and daughters' weddings and it's the decent thing to do. So please, tell your parents that there's really only room for them to invite twenty five people. We really cannot have any more."

Bob and I looked at each, dumbfounded. I grabbed the list from her and scanned it quickly. "Mother, you don't even have any of my friends here. How can this be the list?"

My mom looked startled. "But Irene, you'll choose your own bridesmaids. Those are your friends."

"So I'm allowed to invite four or five people and you get to invite everyone else? Whose wedding is this?" I was livid.

"Irene, I've planned the entire wedding for you. We're paying for the entire wedding. And this is the thanks I get? I should figure that. All my life, everything's done for Irene and all she can do is ask for more. Well listen, there is something called manners. When people invite you to weddings, you do the same in return or the world turns a cold, cold shoulder against you. You want a cold shoulder the rest of your life?"

"Mom, look," I said, breaking into tears and pointing to the guest list. "These men here are drunks. They're going to get drunk at my wedding and ruin the whole day. Can we at least not have them?"

"We are paying for this wedding," Mom told me again. "We'll invite who we want. You get a dress, bridesmaids and a husband out of the deal," she told me, as if Bob were some sort of booby prize.

But Bob just took my hand. "Mrs. Novak, I'm sorry. Irene and I had some ideas about how the wedding would be and she's disappointed to hear that things will be different. But we're very grateful for all of your help."

"She's not," said my mother, wagging her finger. "She doesn't care that we're paying for the whole thing."

"I know, maybe it doesn't seem that way. Sometimes moms and daughters have a hard time talking to one another. But Irene was just saying last night how happy she is that you've agreed to help with this." My mother looked doubtfully at me, but through my tears, I nodded. I had been telling Bob how surprised I was that she didn't put up more of a fight since I didn't want to marry their farmer. I was happy that it wasn't going to be harder than it already was. Now, Mom was proving me wrong. Now it was harder than it had been. But I saw what Bob was doing, and I gave in to his sense. The trick was to get through the ordeal, and then we would be married, no matter what the wedding was like.

So Mom and I went shopping for the dress together, and yes, outstandingly, she let me pick my own dress. That was enormous of her. She put in her ten cents worth along the way, but left the final choice in my hands. And I picked out a dress that was truly stunning. It felt so grand to be given the freedom of that one choice. She was also wide open to my choice of bridesmaids and so the wedding plans were set.

Until, several months later, when my mom learned that the maid of honor, Shirley, was pregnant. "*Pregnant?*" she demanded. "What will people think when they see a pregnant maid of honor? What kind of future is that going to give your marriage?"

I was confused. "But Mom, she's been married for a year. Everybody knows she's married to the best man. Why *shouldn't* she be pregnant?"

"It's not that she shouldn't be pregnant," Mom insisted. "It's that she shouldn't be pregnant and your maid of honor. Maids of honor *cannot* be pregnant. That's the way it's always been. It's tradition, Irene. You have her, and you're asking for bad luck."

It was the same damn story and I became so agitated that the tears started streaming once more. "Mom, tradition doesn't have to decide your life for you. It's just something that shows the way things have been done. Maybe something that has worked for people. But it's no hard and fast rule. Shirley is an important friend. That's a whole lot more important than tradition."

"What will people say?" asked my Mom. "Tradition is the way it is here. Nobody has a pregnant maid of honor or bridesmaid, Irene. That's why breaking tradition is such a big deal, and that's why Shirley cannot be your maid of honor."

"You're kidding, right? I mean, you're really going to say that she can't be?"

"You'd better believe it. Choose what you like on your own time. I don't care anymore. But don't drag me down with you. We're paying for this wedding and it'll go the way it's supposed to." And believe it or not, I did call Shirley with a broken heart and voice and told her. I guess I could be grateful at least that she took it well and didn't let it ruin our friendship. But you can bet it came between my mom and me. Then again, there was so much already between us, it probably didn't add much to the overall weight. By then, I was indeed resigned to just getting through my wedding, not caring really how it all came down, so I didn't bother pointing out the obvious to my mother when all the men I didn't want at the wedding actually did get drunk and started fighting. It was par for the course by then, and I was just glad to be married to Bob.

Mom continued her controlling ways after the wedding, but was limited because I kept her out of my life as much as I could. We still saw my parents some weekends and they still came to visit from time to time. On each occasion, she worked her sorcery. "Irene," she'd say, "you're not really going to cook your potatoes like that are you? You know, this is why I always tried to teach you how to cook. I guess now you're wishing you had spent more time with me in the kitchen, eh?"

And with housework. And with how to dress. And later, with how to raise my children. Her laundry list of my wrong-doings knew no bounds. "How could you go to that expensive hair salon?" she demanded one day. "You think the world is made of money? You ought to be cutting it yourself at home like I do. But you've just got to go to that salon so everyone can see you coming out, is that it?"

Again, it was the same when I got contacts. She was downright angry about that, said they would ruin my eyes. And water. That's right – water. She was upset that I drank so much because drinking a lot of water would be bad for me. It would fill me up and not leave room for food. I was stupid because I didn't watch the news or read the newspaper. I was out of my element when I was elected president of the Chamber of Commerce. I just wasn't high society, and shouldn't pretend to be. When I made a decision to go back to school and receive my undergraduate and graduate degrees, I was told it was a waste of money. What was I going to do with education? And on. And on. And on. And …

Farm house, hand made by author's father, Reno, Alberta, 1940.

Author's mother and family, when they immigrated from Russia to Canada, 1938.

Ukrainian Greek Catholic Church, Reno, Alberta.

The author ages one and three.

The author age five.

Author sitting, second to left; Margie next on right, 1953.

Author age ten.

Author age thirteen.

Grandparents, paternal on left, maternal on right, 1958, Reno, Alberta.

Author's parents, 1958.

Auhor, age fourteen, with parents.

Camping trip, Irene and Magie, 1963.

Irene at age twenty in 1965.

Irene and Bob, 1966.

Irene and Bob, Wedding, 1967.

Irene, Bob and children, Peace River, Alberta, 1983.

Irene at Avalon, 1994.

Jean at Avalon, 1994.

Jean and Irene, Paris, 2005.

Alexander Novak, tombstone, Reno, Alberta.

Chapter Twenty-Six

Jorge was, I'd like to say, something of a madman. The man's tongue put sailors to shame, which was great for shock value, at first. By the end of our first two weeks, which he controlled almost entirely, I think I had forgotten he was even cursing. I've tamed him down for decency, but you can only clean up a man like that so much.

The only problem was, he didn't really offer anything new. That's what I realized as soon as his program began. He was tackling the infamous 12-step program, which meant, once again, that he was addressing addicts. Well, time to snooze. And I might have, too, except that his voice was so loud. Maybe I'd be able to spend time journaling at night, really figure things out for myself and be sleepy for the day. Then I could snooze despite his voice.

But that first day he boomed, and I'd had plenty of sleep. So try as I might, I wasn't getting away with ignoring everything he said. "Selfishness!" he cried out. I think that woke up all the night owls who'd barely made it to breakfast. "Selfishness. Self-righteousness. Self-centeredness. Which one of these, or which ones, make up every day of your life? You, you, you" he said, pointing randomly into our group. "You think you're different, don't you? Think you're something goddamned special. *I'm not selfish. I'm not self-righteous. I'm not self-centered.* Yeah, sure. Half the people coming here figure someone else is the problem. Half of you think someone else should be in your seat. Don't you? Ok, everyone who figures that, you've at least got the self-righteous thing going, don't you?"

Oh, I loved it. It was so easy to pull this gag. Go up to someone who's never had a drop of alcohol in his life and ask if he has an alcohol problem. "No," he'll tell you. But you've got him trapped. "Denial's the first sign," you tell him. Well duh. It's a stupid trick, and it's what Jorge was pulling. You didn't have any problems that related to the Center. You came just so you could fit in a little better with your friends. I was begging the question. "Which one are you," you've got a problem. Right? No way Jorge. You're not pulling that one on me.

"You've got to understand, people. These are techniques. No one's here to blame you for one of these or another, but no one's going to pretend they don't exist either! You've got to fess up sooner or later, or you're going to be trapped. You want to keep living in the shit hole you're in? Fine by me. Make it all a big waste of time. That's great. But do it on your own shift, because I'm not wasting my own goddamned life in this Center without showing a few of you how to fix your own problems along the way."

He paced furiously at the front of the room. "So what are the techniques for? Protection. Self-protection. That's why I'm not here to blame you. Most of you probably feel you've got excellent reasons to put up those kinds of barriers. But I'm going to tell you something right now, and you'd better listen up. You get quizzed on this later, and I'm not shittin' you. Listen! I will be pissed. Pissed! if you don't know the answer. And believe me" he looked at other staff members sitting in the room who all began nodding, "You do *not* want to see me pissed. I'll make your time here a living hell if you piss me off."

Wow. Very macho. I could hardly believe this guy was trying to pull this on adults. "So here's what you'll be quizzed on," he said, looking stormy. "No matter what your reasons for putting up shields and no matter what kind of shield you've put up, your reasons are not external. You perceive them as external, but it's all … inside … you. Your unhappiness, the whole reason you're here, comes from inside you. You project that and out it goes. You see it in front of you, and suddenly you've got to put walls up. And you do by being selfish, self-righteous, or self-centered. End of story."

Right. End of story. End of listening. I'd heard this a million times from self-help gurus that I liked reading. This point was always a stickler for me because I knew it wasn't true. Was it possible that it happened? Maybe that it happened often, or most of the time? Sure. But I knew it wasn't universal, because my Mom had been a hellion when I was a kid and Dad just let it be. If he wouldn't defend me, then I'd have to defend myself. My walls were self-protection, but they weren't protecting me from me. Mom was a true, outside threat.

And then came the frightening part. The one thing I wanted to figure out here, more than anything else, was my marriage. Bob had done me much good, had been a wonderful husband in many respects. But he had also defined and controlled me, a dynamic that had grown more severe with every passing year. So now, I was feeling absolutely strangled by a man who felt that he knew more of what was right for me than I myself knew. How this happened over the years, I was never quite sure. But it was wrong. There was never a question about that. By slow degrees, Bob gave me more and more direction and showed a vicious disappointment when I did not conform. I needed to know what to do with that. Under that kind of oppression, would I ever fulfill my own life purpose? Or did I need to get out altogether? None of this *it's all my own fault* B.S. I needed to reflect on our relationship as it was and try to understand whether I could operate at all under his influence.

"*You!*" exclaimed Jorge, suddenly looking my way. He seemed to love one-word sentences to catch our attention. "You're agoraphobic. Deathly afraid of coming out from the protection of those walls, aren't you?" He was still looking at me, and I nearly snickered. Yeah, he had my number all right. I didn't know what agoraphobia meant, except by context. I just raised my eyebrows a bit and thought, "You yourself. If we're all just projecting stuff, then you must be the agoraphobic, Jorge old boy." To think my friends had raved about this place. It was all smoke and mirrors. All mind games.

And that's when Jorge brought up the 12-steps and I knew I was in the wrong place. "Listen. We're going to start talking about addictions, but first we've got to break a bad habit. Most of society hears the word addiction and they immediately start thinking about drinking or smoking or drugs. That's about it. But we all have addictions. We are addicted to these defensive strategies that I'm talking about and we put these walls up around us when dealing with just about anything – money issues, spouses, parents, illnesses, or so many other things that we never associate with addictions. But I'll be damned if I've seen a person walk through these doors who wasn't addicted to their own, chosen reactions to whatever life has dished out. We get addicted to these and the only real solid way of breaking addictions is the 12-step program. Some of you are more familiar with this. Some less. We're going through the thing and this is going to be most of your first two weeks here. You don't get this, then you don't get what's wrong – *ever!* – in your life. First step. Admit you are powerless. You have become so accustomed to doing things this one way, you are powerless to stop the momentum. Otherwise, you would have. Years ago. But you know that haven't got the power."

I nodded my head and I think Jorge noticed. He might have thought I was actually picking something up. But in my mind, I was thinking, "Yes, I've got your number. Powerless indeed. That's victim talk and I don't believe in being a victim. Well, maybe a victim of my parents and my marriage, since I didn't do anything wrong in those instances. Got any tricks up your sleeve for those, fine. But don't go calling me powerless. I'm here because I have the power to reflect on my marriage and choose what I want to make of it."

"You've got these defenses," Jorge continued. "And do you know why?" Sure I knew. Because people in my life were aggressive and you have to defend against aggression. "Because you want to control situations and people and that's not how life works. You want to have control, but everyone, in one situation or another, has someone else in control. Your parents when you're young, your minister at church and teacher at school, your spouse in areas where he or she knows more than you, even your children, especially when they're young and can make demands. You want to have the control and yet you so often can't. You feel your control slipping, it feels like aggression and up go the walls. Familiar? Don't lie to yourselves, because I know it is. It's why you're here and it's what you can fix."

Yeah, it was familiar. I saw this kind of thing in a number of my clients, although I'd never really thought of it in these terms. This might be useful after all. Information I could take back to work to help my clients. Okay. Let's turn this into an educational experience. I can handle that, and I'm always trying to provide more value for my clients.

"And do you know what happens when you don't feel in control? You feel that you can't get all the things you need or that you think you need. You feel like your needs are suddenly in someone else's hands and that is frightening. Why should you trust them to provide? What if they don't? Suddenly, you find yourself in a place of fear. What if I don't get enough? This is a fear of scarcity, of not enough. When you're in that place, when you feel that the world will not provide and is thus unsafe, you find yourself desperately needing and latching onto security." Hmm. Yes. This *was* good. I could see why my friends had gotten something from this logical connection of events. It would definitely be of benefit to some of my clients.

"But that's not the end. You following me? Listen, I'm going to sum up, then bring it all together. You've got this desire to be in control. Everyone has this desire to some extent. But we all have outside authority figures in different situations of our lives. We hate giving up control in those situations, yet the more we feel that lack of control, the more we fall into this place of fear – will I be provided for? Will there be enough of what I need? So there's this battle going on between control and scarcity, and this creates a ton of stress inside.

"As this stress builds, there's this need to relieve that stress. We look for artificial stimulation or sedation of our emotions. We want to take control again, this time of our emotions. But we think that if we just change our mood, reality itself is changed. This is an illusion. It doesn't stop the battle between control and scarcity. As long as we don't change that, we have a continued need – an emotional addiction – to changing our mood in some way.

"Often this is through alcohol and drugs, which is selfish, self-centered. It is a temporary feel-good for your self without giving a damn how that affects the people around you. This is also done through personality changes and this has to do with self-righteousness. We become better than other people in a desperate attempt to feel that we are the true authority in all situations. But that can never be a fact. We are simply not built to be the best at all things, to be the one that must run the show. You see how it all feeds in? And there's such an easy solution – easy in words, harder in practice. But it can be done.

You can do it. It's admitting that you're not in control. That you are powerless. That is step one. When you acknowledge that, it immediately begins to relieve some of the stress. And relieving that stress is really key to relieving the emotional need for these disastrous solutions."

Jessica. Herb. Millie. They'd all be able to use this. I could see that plainly enough. I'd help them to make some major changes in their lives.

"Schemes, excuses, resolutions. All hopeless!" Jorge said emphatically. "You've tried them all, haven't you? You've thought, *maybe if I just try harder to get out of the situation, or to find a new solution. Maybe if I put it in writing, or reflect hard enough and see it all from some new angle so that I can blame that angle. Maybe then, things will be fixed.* But you've already looked at it from a million angles. You've blamed a million events and a million people. You've tried harder to fix these problems, but always believing that the problems were outside yourself; so you were trying to change others, even just to change how they felt about you. But this did nothing because you ignored the reality that you are never a victim of circumstance and that you're responsible for your own behavior. Get me?"

Vivian. Henry. Adam. Yes, I got you. All these people were going to see dramatic shifts in their lives. If I put it this way, they would understand. Maybe Jorge wasn't so bad after all. He was hitting the nail on the head for many people's problems, even if mine in fact did originate outside myself. I was starting to get anxious to tell my own life story. The sitting swing. The hailstorm God sent to punish me. The time I was nearly raped and my mom, who heard me screaming, didn't even try to help. Yes, this way, at least the Center could acknowledge that sometimes it started outside a person. But then I'd agree with them that it could be different for others. Things would be happy all the way around.

"When you get to the point where you can see reality the way it is, when you can admit that you are powerless, then you'll have the chance to feel a release and simply accept the grace of God."

Jonathan. Bernie. Sherri … what? Did he say to accept the grace of God? The same God that punished me with hail? That thought my three verses from the Bible were a joke? That forced people into crazy, riverside Baptisms? Grace of God? I didn't think so.

"Admit that you are powerless," Jorge kept saying. "Admit that you are helpless on your own. That you need to surrender. Powerless," he said. "Powerless. Powerless. Powerless."

Chapter Twenty-Seven

After the lecture we were sent to our rooms to write, which is something I'd find myself doing often. Oh, I'd already thought to journal plenty on my own, but I never knew we'd be asked to write so much that would be shared with the staff. Fine. I could handle that. I knew how to write what they should see. So I gave them an earful – all the right kind of introspective nonsense they were looking for.

Later we engaged in role playing, as if we had hit rock bottom in one situation or another and we had to end up acknowledging that whatever we tried had failed and that if there was any solution, it had to be outside ourselves. When I was asked what kind of rock bottom I had hit, I just stared at them. I hadn't hit one at all. Rock bottom had to do with addicts. I could see the counselors were frustrated with me, but what was I supposed to do – just make something up?

So they had me role play a drunk, which had no relation to real life with me. I had an aversion to alcohol ever since my grandfather beat me and a drunk was the last thing I'd ever become. "Oh," I said, to end the session. "I just can't take any more of this getting drunk and puking and blacking out. But ... but ..." I spluttered, putting on a real show, "It's *too damn tempting*. I'll never be able to knock this stupid habit!" I got mixed reviews for my performance. There were a lot of alcoholics there who related all too well. Some were glad for my fine depiction of that moment, but others saw the tongue in cheek and I could tell they were angry. I'd have to apologize to them later, I knew. I would have to tell them it was just my frustration with what I thought were useless ways to find life solutions.

The next day we were back with Jorge once more, and he was on to explaining this higher power. "Thirty two people in this group today. That means thirty two definitions of higher power what we call God without the limitation of my definition or your definition – God as you understand it, God as I understand it, God as each of us understands it. Call it what you will – Spirit, Savior, Energy, Creator, Holy Ghost. Just know what it means for you, and we can simply say *God* or *Higher Power* without having someone else in the group draw back.

"See, we *need* to be able to use these terms, because I know – I *know* – that I made one thing clear yesterday. You have *got* to believe there's something outside yourself. If you don't, then you don't believe there is a solution to your problems, because heaven knows you haven't figured it out for yourself, now have you?"

If you'd let me go to my room and have time to reflect on my own stuff, maybe I would have figured it out by now, I think. But I keep the thought to myself.

"Step one. You notice just one thing. You've failed to find the answer because you've been looking to yourself. But, there is something outside yourself. Something greater. Your God. Your Higher Power. Ok, great.

"Step two. That Higher Power does have the answer and can lead to your happiness. That's all. If you believe in a higher power and you know you don't have the answer, then you'd better start believing that the one thing truly greater than yourself does have those answers. This is the only way you can find hope, you see. Humans aren't going to provide you with any better answers than you were able to provide yourself. But God can do just that. If." He looked around, seeing whether anyone would bother to complete his sentence. *If what?* he seemed to ask us. "If you're willing to turn it all over to Him, Her, It. Whatever – all just labels. You can't just say, *I'm turning over my addiction.* It doesn't work that way. If God can't work through everything about you, He can't change what drives you, what leads you to your addictions. So you've got to turn over more than just an addiction. You've got to turn over your life and your will."

Hmm. Fair enough. This probably applied even to my situation with my husband. Too many years I'd been directed by him, rather than by my own soul's purpose. It made sense that I could achieve a lot more of that purpose if God, not necessarily the one I knew from the Bible, but the good one that so many people talked about, or maybe just my-Soul-as-God was directing me instead. And if I turned things over that way, let this Higher Power lead me, maybe it would lead me right out of my marriage. Maybe it wouldn't. But in any case, I wouldn't let Bob be my leader and director. I would have a higher leader. That didn't sound bad at all. I'd give it a whirl.

Now we're sent to write once more, and I ran with that notion. I know what they want to see, and I'm somewhat willing to give that a try. *I believe I have great possibilities!* I write. *Now that I'm more aware of my ego, my identity, and the workings of both, I can live a more loving life, one day at a time. I also see becoming more spiritual on a daily basis. I believe that my Higher Power is the solution. Yes! Surrender, believe, and achieve. I truly believe in a Higher Power. I am peaceful, joyous, loving, and feeling surrendered. My life is finally becoming happy, calm, and content.*

Good. Good. I'd have them buttered up. And I felt ok about it, because it was all true in a sense. I was ready to make that surrender. It sounded nice. If they could just give me the free time I was really hoping for, I could start to make it happen and listen inside myself, to my Higher Power of course – for answers to my situation.

"*Bullshit!*" Jorge yelled when we got back into session that afternoon. "What the f– do you think this is, some college psych class? You think we don't see through this kind of shit?" He grabbed a stack of our papers off a desk near the front of the room, waved them violently, then threw them into the air. They cascaded all around him. "Who the f– do you think I am? Some moron who doesn't have anything better to do than waste his time on dribble? '*I know my Higher Power now,*'" he mocked. "'I'm a perfect person now because of your two lectures. Thank you so much Jorge, you've changed my silly little life. My Higher Power is now in control. I'm surrendered. I love life.'" He stared daggers at us. "What the f– is that? You think I'm going to buy that you've turned your whole life around in two days because I've given you the first two steps of twelve and you haven't had a day to make them real." Boy oh boy oh boy. You could hear a pin drop on the carpet. No one was looking at Jorge. Not even me. Part of me wanted to think things like "Serves you right for giving us second grade information." But no, I couldn't even think that sarcastically. He had seen right through what I wrote and what everyone else wrote. We were all in this fix together. "Get the f– out of my sight," he said, his voice finally lower but more painful than ever.

Jorge walked out of the room. None of us even wanted to look at the others sitting around us. A counselor walked quietly into the room and gave us a minute to sweat it out. "Two hours," he told us. "You've got two hours to park yourself somewhere and write. From *inside*," he emphasized. "Don't try pulling the same stuff on Jorge twice. It is not a pleasant twenty eight days if Jorge is angry with you." I walked out of the room, as everyone else, working furiously in my mind to think of what to write. Two hours later I returned to the class with a blank sheet of paper. I just didn't know what to write. Jorge didn't even look at the papers before continuing on to step three. I wonder, when he did look the thing over, if just maybe he thought it was a more honest appraisal than the first had been.

Chapter Twenty-Eight

"It doesn't do you a *damn* bit of good to recognize the mess you're in and you won't do a thing about it," said Jorge. He didn't say a thing about our writing failures before and hadn't had time to read the new stuff we'd written. He just got into things as if none of that had happened. "This Higher Power's got the answers, right? So what? That doesn't do a thing unless you'll turn it all over to that power. And turning it over all comes down to will. Now, whose will am I talking about?" He looked over us, energized as always. "Whose will?" he asked again. "You," he said, pointing to a young man near the front of the room. "Whose will am I talking about?"

"Well, my own I guess."

"Why? Why would I be talking about your will?"

The young man shifted uncomfortably. It was almost certainly one of those rotten situations when a teacher has a specific answer in mind, and unless you happen to nail it, you're wrong. Even if your answer has merit. "Because my will decides whether I'll turn things over to my Higher Power?"

"Damn straight," said Jorge. "Sort of." Sort of? That was a good one. Jorge was going to prove me wrong. He gave some credit to the answer while having something else in mind. Good for him. "When I say that this has got to do with will, I'm talking about your will, and I'm talking about God's will, and I'm talking about which one *you* want running the show. Now, unless you want to shock me by proving that you're already enlightened in which case I'll turn this whole Center over to your care, unless you want to show me that, then I can tell you already what your entire will revolves around. It's all about basic human needs. In a way, we've talked about your needs before. You spent your life using different defenses and being *addicted* to those defenses because you had to satisfy certain needs. Those defenses could be your addictions to substances or your general coping skills with those around you.

"But let's talk about those needs, because understanding them is going to give you a window inside yourself. We get this straightened out, you're going to start having a new perspective on *why* you put certain defenses into place. That's going to help us with our third step here, and it's going to get you where you need to go."

He paused, glancing through the crowd. It's when I realized that I was giving him my attention, rather than my attitude. Funny, I wasn't expecting that. He looked at me in that moment and locked eyes. Then, I know it, I saw just the slip of a smile at the very edge of his lips. He looked away and continued, pacing back and forth across the front of the room as he spoke.

"Human needs. We've all got them. The question is all about how we fulfill them. Some of you may already know about Maslow's *Hierarchy of Needs*. I'm going to talk about a similar concept, though this was developed by William Glasser. This is what he explained. Our most basic need is survival. After that comes love and acceptance, then power, or recognition, then freedom and finally fun. We all have to fill all of these needs, and what you have to start looking at is what your needs are in each of these areas.

"See, the picture in my mind and your mind when I mention fun is very different, isn't it? Same with any of these. Survival for one person may literally conjure images of scraping food from trash cans. For someone else, it may make an image of struggling to pay the bills on a BMW. The BMW, in this case, of course also plays a part in love and acceptance, power or recognition, freedom, and fun, doesn't it? A car like that is a means of filling many needs at once, at least as you perceive your needs. I'd like us all to stay in here to write for this next project, half an hour only. I'd like you to write or draw what you feel your needs are for each of these five areas." Jorge stepped back and grabbed a poster from the wall that had been turned away from us. He showed it to us, and scrawled across in bold, black letters were each of these needs. He hung this on the wall at the front of the room. "Cover each category of needs," he reminded us. And we got to work. My own writing came out swiftly:

Survival Needs: the basics, but not in the streets. A roof over my head, food to eat, money to pay the bills. I was raised in a home without electricity or plumbing, so when it gets down to needs, I don't include those even if I definitely prefer them. Money to pay the bills can mean quite a simple home. Food, however, should be more than just sustenance to get you through another day. It should be healthy food, which sometimes costs a little more, but keeps you healthy and energized a lot longer – so healthy food is a matter of long-term survival.

Love and Acceptance Needs: It's important for me to have people around to love, and who can return that love. But to fill my needs, this doesn't just mean a family who's physically present. Most people have a family of one type or another, but that doesn't mean they are being properly loved. We express real love when we help those around us to fill the other needs on this list. And others share real love when they help us to fill our own human needs.

Power or Recognition Needs: I don't need to be recognized by others for anything special about myself, but I do need to have the power to fulfill my life purpose of teaching and promoting spiritual living. If someone tries to take that power from me, they are acting against my very soul's purpose.

Freedom Needs: This ties in with the point above. I am happy to give up a lot of my time to help others and to meet my daily obligations. But I need to also have the freedom of expression so that I can pursue things that will fulfill my soul's purpose.

Fun Needs: Fun fun fun. What is fun for me? Really, what is fun is what makes me feel full. I thrive on happy moments with friends and family as anyone does. But as far as fun needs, even those moments are not as happy as they could be if I feel that I am lacking in the power or freedom to pursue my goals. If anyone threatens those, then I cannot really experience a deep joy in anything, because there is something lacking in the deepest part of me.

As I finished this up and looked back over it, I realized this little exercise was revealing. Almost too revealing, because when I thought about it, this spoke about a great deal of my life. My survival needs were quite basic, and because they were so well met, didn't exactly drive my daily actions. But what about the others? What I had written about love and acceptance spoke directly about my struggles with my parents and with Bob. In particular, my mother for all those years had never really put my hand to anything because she thought I did things the wrong way, and told me so. I was given no power to do things on my own. Although I gained more freedoms with my years, these were slow in coming and seemed to be based on my mother growing weary of her watch more than with her interest in giving me room. Fun was tied in with that, because fun as a kid meant having freedom to play and explore. When I was too old to be kept from playing with Margie, that finally opened to me. It hadn't been encouraged much in our home.

The pattern felt that it was repeating in my marriage. Survival needs weren't much of an issue. But over the years, what felt like love in the beginning of marriage felt more and more like prohibition. In all these years, I had never achieved what seemed to be my soul's unique purpose of teaching. Bob had drawn a boundary inside of which I was meant to dwell. Raising the kids was acceptable, and so was working. But to reach out, to risk in order to fulfill my dreams, this was not something a family could depend on and was not a decision that I was allowed to make. In the end, this meant that I could enjoy the fine moments of family and friends to a degree, but never deeply, never in a way that would really quench my thirst for fun, as Glasser put it. I wondered at this point whether I should even share what I'd written with the staff here at the center, but as I looked it back over, I knew that none of the details could be known from just that sheet of paper. So I would turn it in after all, but would keep the revelations to myself.

Chapter Twenty-Nine

"So you've gotten a glimpse into your needs," Jorge told us when our half an hour was up. "Those are the needs of your will. But now I have a question for you: do those needs represent the will of your God, your Higher Power?" He took a few paces, then stopped and stroked his chin. *How to put it?* he must have been thinking. I didn't think people really stroked their chins when thinking, but he made it look completely natural. "For instance, when we think of things from our own little wills, we often try to fill our needs with details that make us feel successful, accomplished, and somehow greater than those around us. We want that car to make us powerful. We need that elite group of friends to feel that we belong. That's not to put us down. It is human nature to want to feel special. But God is not human. So what is God's will? Does God care if you do this or that? Or does God focus on why you're doing things and how you do them?

"If your Higher Power asked you to forget all your ambitions and to focus only on why you were doing anything, how would you feel about that? If your Higher Power asked you not to care who approved of you, so long as you were approaching each person in a very loving way, as described by your Higher Power, do you think you could stop caring what people thought?

"These are the kinds of challenges people face when they're looking at whether they should follow their own will or God's. But *you*," he said, pointing out across us all, "you have an advantage. You already realize that following your own will has gotten you nowhere. You already know that you'll never break the habits that keep you from really feeling full. So why would you want to keep going after these images that you fantasize will bring you happiness? This takes us back to our steps. First, you acknowledge that there *is* a Higher Power. Next, you believe that this Higher Power has the answers you're looking for, because you know that *you* certainly don't have those answers. That just leaves us with the leap. Are you going to turn your will over to God and live by God's will? Are you willing, so to speak, to stop willing and to start following a Greater Will, a Higher Power?

"You," he said, walking briskly across the room to an older lady on the other side. I could tell she was nervous and hoping that he wasn't really looking her way. But he stopped right in front of her. She just looked up with her mouth barely agape. "What do you think? Ready to turn your life over to God? Ready to get things back on track?"

"Well," said the old lady, a little quiver in her voice. Yeah, I felt badly for her. "That is why I'm here," she told him. "I'm here to find out what the answers are and do what it takes. So yes, I'm ready to turn my will over to God."

"Seriously?" asked Jorge. "That's pretty amazing, because I bet you haven't even thought about what God's will is, have you?" The woman looked down. "I bet *none* of you have thought about that. How on earth are you going to turn things over if you don't know what the answers are on the other side? You turn your will over, and then what are you going to do? Sit on your asses the rest of the day since you've got no will? No no no," he said, wagging his finger. "We're not going to let that happen." And out came the sheets of paper. "What is your Higher Power's will for you? Minimum thirty minutes on this, but we've got three hours till dinner and I want you using as much of that time as possible. Without this, you haven't got a life to start living once you turn things over. You've got to have a life worth looking forward to. And remember, that doesn't mean deciding what you think your Higher Power should will for you. Step outside yourself. Figure it out. What does the Higher Power really want? And here's the trick," he added. "You need to write the answer in your non-dominant hand first. Then copy your answer in your dominant hand. That's your assignment. I'll see all of you tomorrow."

Jorge left the room and we were to sit and write. At least half an hour. That was funny, because I really had already written about this before. My soul wanted me to help teach and heal others and promote spirituality. That was simple enough. Would it really make any difference to write things in my non-dominant hand first? I picked up my pencil and starting to write. *The will for me is to be the best I can possibly be moment by moment. To understand God as my Higher Power, my Creator, and the Source for all my needs. To be connected to the Source and to believe in order to create love.* I wrote it again in my dominant hand.

It was the simplest thing in the world to write, but something happened as I penned that final period. A shift. And I wrote my thoughts. *Wow! I just finished writing this in my dominant hand and I had the most incredible feeling of surrender and closeness to God. Wow! This is my spiritual awakening – for today.* It was true. I really felt that way. I knew the counselors were going to love this. I couldn't wait for their reaction the next day. After my half an hour was up, I excused myself and went on a walk until dinner.

○

Of course you already know what happened. Next day came and not a word. Nothing. Jorge kept lecturing, we kept writing and none of the counselors approached to say a lick about what, for me, was a real experience

– something deep, moving, something that had an impact on me in a place where I'd hoped to have no impact from what they were doing, only because I wanted to be right about the place. Here I was, boldly admitting I was wrong, that I *could* learn something here. And they didn't give me an ounce of recognition. So that night, I spend some time writing in my room, scrawling madly across the page and not caring what kind of mess my notes looked like.

I'm confused, angry, rejected, and lonely. I want to be heard. I want the opportunity to be heard. Ever since childhood I was never given the opportunity to express my needs and wants and to tell my story. Even here I feel that no one wants to listen. It seems that as soon as I start talking, the person that I'm talking to turns off or doesn't let me finish, but starts into their own story. I have a story too. I want to talk to people. I want to be heard.

In one week, not one person has asked me to go for a walk with them. I go for three walks a day and I always ask if anyone wants to join me. No one does. My parents didn't want to hear me when I was growing up, and they still don't want to hear me. I got married and my in-laws don't want to hear me. My husband shuts me off when I express my needs and feelings. I come here and it's the same thing. It's a lonely feeling. Last night when we were all planning a breakfast, I had some ideas but it was so loud and chaotic, not one of my thoughts was heard. The loud ones dominate, and I am left behind.

I'm confused about going within – to me, this means meditation, and Jorge has told us "no meditation." Pretty difficult because we've obviously got different terminologies. I asked my roommate, Gabby, about what he meant, and when she explained what she understood, it sure sounded like meditation again. So I'm lost.

Since I'm not supposed to meditate, I've stuck with strict thinking. I'm doing everything in my head. I've tried talking with people here to understand how they see me and I just get confusing answers. I listen, and I don't know what I'm hearing. Rather than addressing the question, they just go into their stories and their issues. I don't get it.

I've had some thoughts tonight. Of suicide. The way I figure it, what the hell? Not a damn person to hear me out. Rejected everywhere I turn – even the supposedly safest place of all, here at Avalon. So for me, there's only one meaning to it all, and that is that I've got no worth. No worth. It's the only way to explain it at all.

I looked down at the page and a single tear dropped onto it. I put my pen down and turned off my light, then slipped into bed and fell asleep.

Chapter Thirty

The idea of suicide was floating around somewhere inside, but I wasn't so desperate yet that I was ready to attempt it. I slept that night, fitfully, falling into dreams and more restful sleep in the very early hours and somehow I woke up refreshed. The sun was streaming in through my window and it wasn't yet time for breakfast. I couldn't wait for my morning walk. Screw everyone here – if they didn't want to join me for walks, that was fine. I had asked on day one and no one wanted to join me, and I'd had an enormously insightful walk on my own. I asked on day two and day three and started questioning whether I was rubbing people the wrong way. I asked every day since then and came to realize that I was an outsider even amidst this rather pitiful crowd.

So screw them. This morning was beautiful and I would enjoy it. I wouldn't ask anyone to join me. I didn't want them along. I just threw on a light sweater for the nip I knew would be in the air and I headed out into the lounge, toward the door, ready to indulge in being on my own. And that's when I heard someone call my name. I could hardly believe it when I turned and saw who it was. She hadn't been here for the first week of Avalon because she'd been here before. Veterans like her didn't need all the intro material. She was here for a refresher.

That someone was Jean. I knew of Jean because we had common friends and they often spoke of her. However, I had no idea what she looked like. When I looked at the face behind the voice, I immediately recognized seeing her at church..

Church? Oh yeah, I'd seen her at church a couple times too. But the fact is, she never belonged in a church. Anyone would tell you that. If you've seen those spiky hairdos on a girl, like all she can think to do is poke you to death when she gets the chance, and you've seen her struttin' her stuff in a leather jacket, then you know Jean. You know why she didn't belong in a church. People didn't go to church for that kind of environment. I sure didn't.

So it doesn't take much imagination to guess how I felt when circumstance ran us into each other at church one day. I was with my good friend Claudia, who for some reason that was beyond me, loved Jean to death. So she was dousing Jean with this great big hug and as she let go, there was this awkward moment – to hug, or not to hug? Jean didn't know who I was and I didn't know this was *the Jean* my friends spoke so highly of. It wouldn't have been wrong. And if I didn't hug her, was it a point-blank "screw you"? I didn't want to deal with the kickback that that might bring me. I gave Jean a hug – *God, her spiky hair rubbed against my cheek; I hated it!* I nodded at her as we released. She and Claudia spoke for a minute, and then we were off on our separate ways.

That was Jean. My "Avalon" friends mentioned her a lot when they talked about the center since some of them had attended with her. So really, I should have felt confident I'd never see her here. Why would you be here again unless the center didn't work? Score one point for me. For the few patches of light I'd seen here, it looked like my overall suspicions about this place would be confirmed.

So here was Jean, sitting by a table. She looked like she was getting ready to go for a walk as she leaned over to tie up her runners. But was it really her? She wasn't wearing a leather coat and I didn't know when she changed her hairstyle, but it wasn't spiky anymore. Still, I was guarded. Prejudice aside, I was realistic. As a therapist myself, I had a lot of experience with people and knew the personality that went with spikes and leather. Chip on her shoulder, right about everything. It was hard enough just saying hello to someone like that.

Then there was another matter that fit right in. Go figure, after a lifetime with my mother, I was slow to trust women. Men were easy, generally a whole lot more straightforward. With women, there were always hidden nuances and usually some sort of competition going on. I didn't need that. It seemed so childish to me. And it was the kind of thing I'd suffered for too many years with my mom, who always said one thing and meant another if she was smiling, who was always competing by comparing how she did things to the way I did them, and who was otherwise a terror in those moments of violence when she no longer contained what she was really feeling. So far as I was concerned, most of the women I knew showed these characteristics to one degree or another, and I wasn't going to waste my time dealing with them. I'd already lost too many years to those games.

So here was my challenge. What do you do in the face of someone who's calling for you, obviously ready for a walk? Did I face an entire walk with her? Or could I avoid the walk with another awkward hug and a quick nice-to-see-you?

"Irene!" she exclaimed, bounding up to me. "I thought I saw you last night. I can't believe we're here together!" She headed for me, arms extended obviously for a hug.

"I can't believe it either," I told her honestly, though with a little more brightness than I felt.

"Mornings are such an amazing time here. They can really help to clear your head, get you ready for the day. Want to walk together?"

"Of course!" I said. Dumb, dumb, dumb. My stupid instincts for being polite kicked in way too quickly. It was funny, because every morning up till then, I was hoping for someone to join me, though I had only asked the men. But now someone was gleefully asking to join me and I was resisting. *Not a woman and definitely not Jean!* But 'please' and 'thank you' and 'sure you can trample on my personal time and space' are hard habits to break, so I'd given in.

"Come on then," she said taking me by the arm and leading me through the door. "I've got a great path we can take that'll get us back just in time for the first session."

Dumber, dumber, dumber. I didn't like taking planned routes. It was so much more fulfilling and helped me to center myself so much better when I could just meander, following my feet where their whim would take me. I scowled when Jean wasn't looking, then settled into an accepted defeat as we headed down the pathway towards the woods.

"Couldn't stand this place first time I came," Jean told me as we passed beneath the first branches and under the colored canopy. "I thought everyone here was pompous and that everyone here was out to get me. Isn't that funny? I mean, I came here almost against my will but knew that I had to kick some habits. I was miserable, I knew it, yet the last thing I wanted was help from Avalon. It's so crazy to me now."

"Well, I can understand it," I said. "I mean, there's a difference between help and people who think they have all the answers."

"Right," she said, smiling. "Wasn't sure you'd understand. It's so funny because I was busy thinking they were pompous and self-righteous, and really," she laughed, remembering. "Really, I was seeing myself in them."

"Hmm. The old mirror trick," I said wisely. "But you're back. You thought it was worth coming back. Why, if they didn't help you the first time?"

Jean laughed again and looked at me almost quizzically. "Avalon totally changed my life. They helped me in ways I can never explain. You've only been here a week so far and you usually don't get that out of the introductory stuff. I didn't come back because I'm still screwed up, but because I know they can help me with other issues, things that are more subtle, you know?" I wasn't sure that I did. "When you learn how to reflect on your life the way you do here, boy, a light goes on and you're never the same again. So I've been able to see a whole lot more that I want to work on."

"Didn't they teach you how to work on them the first time?"

She shrugged. "Yes, in a lot of ways. But you know, sometimes it's just more helpful to have an extra set of eyes, to have someone else say out loud the things you know and won't even let yourself whisper. Sometimes it's useful to have someone give you permission to change something that you're not sure you deserve to change."

"Why wouldn't you deserve something?" I asked. "If it's about improving yourself, what kind of permission would you need?"

"Have you ever done things because you felt they were right for the people around you? Not just once, but over and over, until you found yourself stuck doing that, no matter what you needed for yourself?" I shook my head, but I didn't like where she was going. I was pretty sure I could relate. "Well, I have. I do it all the time. Not like I used to, but I still find myself getting stuck in patterns that aren't healthy for me."

I stopped right there on the path and she stopped too, turning back to look at me. She raised her eyebrows as if to ask *"What?"*

"That's why I can't stand this kind of pop psychology," I told her. "I don't mean you, but places like this." I didn't want to offend her personally, at least not during our walk. "Sometimes you have to do things for other people, even if it takes a sacrifice on your own part. And there's way too much talk these days about people deciding that isn't what's best for their own growth. So they tell people about how much they need to grow until they find someone sympathetic enough to tell them they should stop sacrificing for other people and start doing what's best just for them. Well can you imagine if everyone started looking out just for themselves? Things would fall apart. We're people. We have to look out for one another or things'll just go to hell." I was probably a little red in the face, but boy, this was a hot one for me. I was sick of people pretending that their own well-being depended on pleasure twenty four hours a day.

Jean was quiet, but she wasn't taken aback at all. She smiled warmly at me and looked right in my eyes. "I really like you, Irene. You're the kind of person who makes this world good and you're absolutely right. We do have to sacrifice for other people. We do have to be there for other people. But have you ever lost yourself in that sacrifice? Have you ever become the sacrifice, rather than a person helping another person? That's what I'm talking about here. Once you reach that point, you can't help people anymore, and if everyone did that there wouldn't be anyone left who could help."

Boy, that was it. This Jean, I couldn't help but like her. She was good. She knew the old *How-to-Win-Friends-and-Influence-People* thing. Tell someone you like them, tell someone they make the world good. Who's going to ignore that? Who can still dislike you after that?

Worse than that, was it possible that she was right? Was it possible that once-spiky-haired, once-leather-jacketed punk girl Jean understood the difference between sacrifice and becoming someone's doormat, or someone's expectation? We were still standing there on the path, looking at one another. And I opened my mouth to speak. Quietly. "You're right Jean." There. I said it. Could hardly believe that I was saying this sincerely to her, but I was. And what's more, the next thing I said was sincere too. "And I like you Jean. I'm glad you're here." She walked up and gave me a hug and this time, it wasn't at all so bad.

We then turned to continue back down the path and we spoke for a little while about Avalon. "You've been with Jorge up till now," she said. "Eventually, you start working with the other counselors and I have to tell you, they are very genuine people, even if you don't like someone's personality. Don't let that part get to you. The techniques they use, work. That's what's important." And everything she said seemed to have one goal – to give me a positive impression of the place, to open me up to what was there. And I was just starting to believe when her focus shifted and landed squarely on me. "So Irene, here I am talking and talking. I'd rather know more about you."

I smiled an easy smile. "Mother, therapist, avid reader," I began. " I love Og Mandino, Wayne Dyer and ...." She stopped me.

"No, I mean about you. Not what you do, but who you are. What is your life purpose? What is your life passion? Why are you here? What do you hope to find?"

What was she doing? This was way too big for a walk in the woods. This was volumes of materials, countless hours of intimate talking, examining every facet of my life. Try to answer this in fifteen minutes, you were looking at all sorts of misunderstanding, all sorts of half-truths. It meant explaining in detail everything I'd reflected on during my first walks alone. But there's a big difference between remembering things, which can happen in seconds, and telling someone, which can take hours and hours to get at all below the surface.

Worse than that, though, was the fact that I was making this escape to Avalon to question my very own life. Why was I with my husband? Why was I not pursuing my life purpose, my life passion? If I told her what those were, she would ask why I wasn't following them. If I mentioned my husband, she would tell me to get away from him. And if anyone was going to tell me that, I had to be the one. I would resent forever someone who felt they could prescribe that kind of thing, especially when they would never know the whole picture. Bob wasn't a bad guy but he had too tightly controlled my life, or I had allowed him to do that. I didn't want Jean taking on an advising role that she hadn't earned.

Knowing me meant knowing it all. Scenes flashed quickly through my mind again about my life, the way I'd reflected on it just a week before.

Those images in mind and the woods that surrounded us made me remember my hours in the woods looking for a baby, and even my desperate attempts to cough up a baby. I snickered.

"What's so funny?"

"Have you ever tried to cough up a baby?" I asked. She gave me a puzzled look, and I grinned. "Don't worry about it." We continued on through the woods, walking as if aimlessly, even though Jean had us on a definite course. I thought I had changed the subject, but I was wrong.

"So, what about you?" she asked again. "Your dreams. Your ambitions. What you hope to get out of Avalon."

"It's such a big question, isn't it?" I asked in return, rather than responding directly. "Probably some of the answer will come to me while I'm here."

"I bet you're right. But when you signed up for Avalon, was there something you wanted to improve? An area of your life you wanted to make better? Most people wouldn't just come here to decide *something* was missing or wasn't working. Usually they have something specific in mind."

She was really pushing. It was a matter of telling her I didn't know, or I didn't want to talk about it. Or lying. But I'd spent all of my childhood with a mother who made up an unreal world, covered things up and wanted me to do the same. I hated lying. I hated playing word games the way I felt so many women did. Telling her I didn't know was somewhat the truth, but maybe not something she wanted to hear. So I gave her the other option. "You know, Jean … I think it's just got to come out in these sessions. I think I've got to find ways to put it into words. But I know that something is out of place." As far as I knew, it didn't have anything to do with what Avalon could solve, although I'd gained some insights so far. But Jean didn't need to know that.

I was happy that she backed off then, acknowledging my need for time. And what do you know? I felt I had actually made a friend now at Avalon. A friend, and surprisingly a *woman*, that I felt I could trust. That seldom happened so quickly, but Jean played none of the usual games. She was apparently there just showing interest in me and offering support. What a find! For the next three weeks, I would have someone I could confide in, ask questions of, and share the experience with. But was the experience worth sharing? She seemed so turned around by Avalon, just as many of my friends had been. Was it possible I could get something here in twenty eight days?

We had taken a roughly circular route and soon emerged from the woods, not far off from where we entered and soon we were back in the Center. As with most of my other morning walks, we were there in time to grab some food and head into our first session of the day. And there, Jorge stood front and center once more and continued on his tirade. With Jean at my side now, I was a little more open to the experience. *Let's see if this guy is really just a windbag, or if he's got something for me to learn.* As it turned out, there was plenty he could teach me, but that was not the miracle of Avalon.

Chapter Thirty-One

"So, you think you're ready do you?" asked Jorge. "You think you know what your Higher Power is asking of you. You know you've screwed things up, you might as well try God's way, right?" Nobody dared to nod. It was an obvious trap. But Jorge stopped his pacing and looked at us, raising his eyebrows. "Well now, from everything you've written, I figure you guys have your Higher Power all figured out and I know you said you're ready to take that step. Do you want to be off drugs for good? Off alcohol? Off any of your other patterns of behavior?" We nodded tentatively as a group.

He spread his arms out wide. "Good!" he said, beaming. "Only thing is, we've got to have you ready for that change. I mean, I know you want to get out of whatever little private hell you've created for yourself. I was in a shit hole at one time too, remember. I know what it's like, and you can't wait to get out. So you stop drinking, or you stop living your life for other people, or you stop whatever ridiculous thing you might have been doing and suddenly, your relationships with other people change. The problems you've been facing change. And that's good news. But then, something else opens up. A new challenge. And what is that?"

He looked casually around the room, waiting for anyone to raise a hand. " Jean, welcome back," he said suddenly. Everyone turned to face Jean, who blushed. "Folks, if you haven't met Jean yet, please say hello sometime today. She wasn't with us for the first week because this is a return visit for her, something we welcome all of you to do in the future. You get to avoid all my harassing for the first week but come back to gain a little more from the group interaction and from the counselors. Of course that means, like Jean, you've got all the answers. So why don't you cheat for them, Jean. What challenge do you face once all these ugly problems start disappearing."

Jean cleared her throat and smiled. "Well, drinking, drugs, or whatever addictive behavior you've got isn't the root of everything that's going on. It's a symptom of something deeper. Probably you guys already talked about that, didn't you?" Jorge nodded. "So once you're rid of the symptom, you have to deal with the cause."

"Bing!" said Jorge, tapping his finger to his nose. "You got that? No more artificial pain relief. You got a headache, no aspirin. You've got to figure out why you're getting headaches. So you stop drinking coffee rather than treating the thing with aspirin. Same with this. No more drinking to take away your pain. You've got to figure out what's causing the pain. No more running madly around trying to please the people around you so you don't have to deal with their displeasure. You've got to figure out why someone else's displeasure affects you so powerfully that you would spend your life avoiding it. Was someone angry enough with you all your life that you were abused? Think that had something to do with living to please others today?

"Or maybe you spent your childhood feeling neglected and then, getting out into the so-called real world, you found that people in general didn't give a rat's ass about you. They were all caught up in their own lives. So you figured the neglect you faced as a child wasn't by chance. You really just weren't worth a damn. You picked up a beer and never looked back. It was the only way to forget that you weren't worth anything. And of course you were wrong. You were worth plenty, but circumstance made you think differently. So that's where you have to go back and change your belief. You see? It's not about getting rid of the symptom. It's about removing it so that you can go after the root.

"So your next steps are going after those roots and admitting them out loud – first, to yourself and your Higher Power, and eventually to the group. You have got to find that root cause, and with it, your fault in the process that led to your current behaviors. That doesn't mean that you were at fault for your father drinking or your mother selling herself or your uncle beating you. It means that you were responsible for how you interpreted those events and how you then responded to them. Roots. Reactions. Roots. Reactions. Got it?

"Now listen to me. Listen up!" Jorge looked carefully around the room to make sure he had us. He wanted every eye on him. "Plenty of you have thought you were looking for these roots and reactions for the longest time. But if you'd found them and identified them correctly, you wouldn't be in the mess you're in. So you have got to knock off your God damned rationalizing. I'm the one God damned person in all the world who isn't at fault for my problems," he mocked. And ow! It stung. "I couldn't have responded any differently. I never asked for any of it. Everyone treated me the same way, so there could only be one explanation. Bullshit!" He threw his arms into the air. "A whole family can treat you the same way because they were all raised the same way, the father and all your uncles and aunts and even their parents, for instance. And then you think the whole world views you as worthless, even though most the world thinks you are average or even terrific. So get over all those damn excuses you've used all these years. They ain't getting' you nowhere! Honest inventory," he told us. "Honest inventory. Roots. Reactions. Roots. Reactions."

Jorge motioned to the counselors, who started to haul out the paper once more, but one of them approached him and held a quick and quiet conversation. "Ah," said Jorge aloud. "A most excellent point. "Thank you Joan." He clasped his hands behind his back and paced for a moment, then stopped and planted his feet firmly, facing us. "How many of you have got ambitions? Big ambitions? Going to change the world?"

I looked around quickly. God knew I did, but I also didn't want to find myself raising my hand alone. Luckily a number of people raised their hands, so I raised mine. "Good. Thank you," said Jorge. "I'd like you to calmly walk over to the window and throw them out." We all looked in confusion at one another. Was he serious? "Not literally," said Jorge, to answer the unspoken question. "But you'd damn well better do it. All your ambitions – out the window. Now. Forever. You got it? There's not a person in this world who can keep his own, personal ambitions and still his will over to God. Not one person. If God has ambitions for you, that's fine. But let them be God's ambitions. You're not here to be ambitious. You're here to fix your problems by living God's will for you. So say good-bye to your ambitions. You're going after roots and reactions here. This is your inventory of yourself, understanding what drives you. But if you've got ambitions driving you, you're not going to make an honest inventory. Ambitions color every thought about how we need to be, how we need to portray ourselves. They cloud true vision. Let those go right now or you're in for it. You'll never find the real solution to your problems. Think I'm kidding? All I can say it, doubt me and you'll fail here, You'll fail for the rest of your life until at last, you decide that ol' Jorge was right."

Teaching, Healing, Promoting spiritual values. These were Godly ambitions. They were not little "me" ambitions. And these Godly ambitions were enormous, because my sense of purpose was enormous. My sense of how many people I could help, how many I could heal and guide. Throw that out the window, and you might as well be throwing out my soul. If Jorge thought that would mean more health for me, he didn't know my relationship with God. He didn't know that God had given me my ambitions. I would write a bit about my childhood and he would finally start to see. My ambitions now didn't have a thing to do with what happened way back then.

Chapter Thirty-Two

Jorge walked into the room the next day with his hands to his head, just about pulling out his hair. He looked at us wildly, hands still in place up there. "What do I do with you guys? What am I supposed to do?" His hands went up high into the air as if to ask the question, then they dropped back to his side, fists clenched. "Inventory," he told us. "*Inventory!* We're not here to explain what happened. Frankly, I don't give a damn that your father made you smoke cigarettes or that you caught your uncle watching you get dressed or even that your mother beat you. Those are all just things that happen. They're God-awful things, we all know that. But they're events that take place *outside of you*. And it doesn't do me a damn bit of good to know about those things without knowing what you felt and how you reacted. Those are our keys. What happened inside you. Because the whole world, as far as you're concerned, is how you perceive it – what you think, believe, feel, experience.

"But this," he said, holding our papers up in front of us once more. "This is bullshit. These are events, and I told you I didn't want events. Hey, I can guess that you were scared when your dad was coming after you with a belt. I'm sorry as hell that it happened. But not because you were beat so much as because it drove you into reactions that led you eventually into addictions. You've got to figure out what those reactions were, because those reactions are your fault.

"Did you hear me? I said those reactions are your fault! You might not have ever asked someone to beat you or rape you or be a lousy parent. But those offenders never demanded that you react one way or another. Only you can control that. What changed inside you when you dealt with all of that? We have to get you past that, get you back to the reactions you naturally had to life when you weren't dealing with one ungodly event or another."

It was funny. Jorge was a crackpot and made sense at the same time. I resented that he felt I had any fault at all about how I was raised, but I couldn't argue that reactions took place inside me. It seemed wrong that you could put any fault at all on a child who didn't know any better way to react, so I wanted to lash out at Jorge. But at the same time, did he really mean the kind of fault you should feel guilty about? I was pretty sure he was just talking about responsibility, since no one else could determine my reactions, no matter how young I was.

Jean continued sticking by me at every break we had, walking with me, talking. She was fantastic – really! She would listen to some of my own challenges with the center and, increasingly, with my own life, and you know, she never told me what I should do. She never suggested I should make one decision or another. All she did was relate things to struggles she had gone through, and she'd tell me how she dealt with each. This was the nicest approach anyone had used with me, because there was no sense of judgment or superiority. Just two people being present with each other, and in support of one another. I could hardly believe I was experiencing this with a woman. The only other woman I'd ever really trusted hadn't been so much a woman as just a wise, young girl named Margie. But after graduation, Margie headed east and we were only in touch once in a while.

So here was Jorge, making sense and yet repelling me, and I didn't know how to react. I felt that, even when I had a kind of breakthrough here, I was still not acknowledged except by Jean. I still doubted whether Avalon could bring any real healing at all, even though I was starting to understand more and more that there was some healing to do. I looked a few seats to my left where Jean sat, wondering whether I should be here. Jean only looked back and smiled a pure and simple smile which set me at ease. She was good at that, I found. What a surprise she was, over and over again.

Jorge was waving more sheets of paper at the front of the room and as I tuned in, I realized he was handing out a questionnaire. It was supposed to help us do our inventory again, only this time with more success. "No butterballing," Jorge told us. "One of the toughest things to do is admit emotions and reactions you're ashamed of for some reason. But if you can't say it out loud, you're never going to be able to face it. On behalf of addicts everywhere, I can tell you that this is more or less a universal truth, you got it? No changing things because you're afraid of who might read it. This is it, folks. Live or die here. It's your choice."

No changing things for the reader. I see. If he thought I trusted the counselors I'd seen around here, that was a laugh. But it might not be bad to share with Jean. That might make sense. So I'd write things down, but let's see what I'd do from there. "Two days," I suddenly heard. I shook my head, confused. What was two days? "You've got two days to fill this out. I expect it to be thorough and to show some deep, deep reflection. Live or die – but at least you've got two days to decide."

Holy mackerel! He thought it would take two days to answer a few questions? I scanned them quickly: *What or who do you resent? What causes you to feel resentful? How has this resentment affected the way you think, feel, and behave? Which character traits are active? I resent _____ because _____. This affects _____. This activates _____ _____.* Two days? Fair enough. Lots of time to journal on my own. Maybe a few extra long walks across the beautiful area.

I headed to my room, glad as always that Gabby didn't spend any time here. Solitude. It was the bliss I needed. My escape. I looked at the sheet and started writing easily.

I resent my husband because he doesn't listen when I try to tell him what my needs are. This affects my self-esteem. This activates my anger. Ha! See? Piece of cake. Jorge was a nut for giving us two days, but I wouldn't balk. I always loved getting work done ahead of time and then being free. *I resent my mother because I can never please her. This affects my self-esteem. This activates my fear of rejection.* This was good stuff. And I paused on reading it again. I noticed that I jotted down "self-esteem" twice. That was funny, because I was totally confident in myself. I had one of the highest self-esteems I knew of and most people around me would agree. But did I?

I shook the question from my head and continued to write. And write. And write. I had two days – might as well enjoy the quiet time to explore inside. It was one of my favorite things to do anyway. I spent more than an hour writing non-stop, then took a break for reflection, joined Jean for a walk, came back and wrote some more. Reflection. Walks. Two days of all this. And all the while, I couldn't really shake that stupid question away for good.

Self-esteem. I had loads of it. I knew that. So why couldn't I convince myself after writing those two ridiculous little sentences?

Chapter Thirty-Three

I'd heard a lot about something called "the Hot Seat" from my friends who'd gone to Avalon. It was the moment you were put on the spot – something I always figured came at the end of the twenty eight days, since by then you had things figured out and you had to be tested on your knowledge and your resolution. But after our two days for writing, we learned that we would face another two days in the Hot Seat.

The meeting room was reconfigured for this. All chairs in a U with one chair set before the U. Three other chairs faced the one directly. Just glancing into the room was enough to chill the length of my spine. I just knew how intense this was going to be, under the spotlight, nowhere to run.

Well, I thought I knew. But nothing really could've prepared any of us for just how intense it was. And no matter how much I was trying to distance myself from this place with my attitude, no matter how much I thought I knew the things to say to get them off my back, this spooked me. Under the pressure, who knew how I would react?

That morning, I wanted to go on my usual walk before breakfast and arrive back just in time for the session. But when I came to the lobby that morning and saw a few people waddling around the session room, I took a peek and asked if they knew what was going on. One of the counselors said "We're doing the Hot Seat today."

"Oh. That's not so good," I said, as if I knew what I was talking about. I looked back in and started understanding the configuration. A bunch of chairs for your audience. Three for your interrogators. Right. "Yeah, not so good," I said again.

"What do you think will happen?" someone asked. And so began a few conjectures, which, as more people arrived for breakfast, became full-fledged rumors. When Jean showed up, I quickly backed off pretending too much knowledge and let people go after her for the facts. But she was a clam and wouldn't open her mouth. "You'll see in less than an hour," she'd say. And so everyone had to keep with the rumors, just to pass the time.

Anticipation and anxiety mixed into a funny tension by the time we sat down. We held our breaths as they confirmed the general interrogation-with-audience structure. "We'll be asking you questions and you are, of course, expected to answer honestly," explained Jorge. "It's important that you not answer for the sake of the audience, but for your own sake, which means telling the truth. It's the only way we can get to some core issues. You're not here for other people. You're here for you. But it's also important that you express yourself in front of the group. Facing things in front of others is part of the healing process.

"You see, if we only discover something about ourselves in secret, we have no pressure about correcting any problems. When other people are aware, they don't need to exert any pressure. We do that for ourselves. It's a funny thing about human nature – we all know that we're not perfect, but we don't want others to know what our imperfections are. We'll use that to our advantage. The imperfections we're dealing with here are the ones that have made you miserable for years and years. By finding them within a group setting, you'll look forward to correcting it as fast as possible. We've got a little over two weeks left, so hurrying things along sure can't hurt, can it?"

"I don't know, can it?" asked one brave soul near the front of the room, pointing at the Hot Seat. Everyone laughed – even the counselors.

"Maybe just a little," admitted Jorge, smiling. "I'll tell you a little secret. The art of perfecting oneself involves pressure. You can pressure yourself just a little, and over long periods of time, you will improve. If you apply more pressure and I mean positive pressure here, rather than living with a guilty conscience every second you will improve. The more you condense the pressure, the more you'll feel it and the faster you'll improve. Makes sense, right? Remember, it takes enormous pressure to make a diamond. But in the end, it's worth it. That's what I want you all to discover in your process here."

It was funny, but something shifted in me. When someone up front made that single joke, there was suddenly a light feeling to the session – something I'd never really seen in the sessions until then. And with the joke, I saw Jorge laughing – something I also hadn't really seen. And finally, as he painted that beautiful picture of what each person here could become, I'll be damned if I didn't suddenly have a soft spot for him somewhere inside. Maybe I was still a little unsure of his methodology. Maybe I couldn't say that I loved the guy, but suddenly, at least I liked him and respected his work. After all my hesitation about Avalon, this was a surprise and a somewhat welcome one at that.

It was also a good thing to feel when the tension came back in and we were ready to begin. Jorge and two other counselors, Martha and Albert, stood near the three chairs and everyone held their breath as they got ready to call up the first victim. "Evelyn." We all breathed out our relief, except Evelyn, who seemed to quiver on her way up to the chair. And boy, the thing was gruesome to watch. Those counselors, led by Jorge, were brutal, prying in on Evelyn's most awful secrets, fears, and issues. It didn't take long for them to break her into tears, which kept streaming down her face for nearly an hour. At last she was allowed back down, and the next person was called. After around an hour again, another was called and each time, they had the person broken down inside ten minutes, or less. We had breaks along the way, but even the breaks were intense. Those who'd been through it didn't really want to face the rest of us. Those who hadn't were still sweating out the wait.

The end of the day arrived and I hadn't been called. I hurried off to my bedroom. Solitude. God, it felt good! I didn't want the next day to arrive. This was too much for me – definitely not what I came for. If I'd known about the Hot Seat, no one would've gotten me here.

But the next day did arrive and before long they had me in the chair. I would get through, I decided. I would be strong and would give good answers. I would show the other people it wasn't all so bad. I would make it through. As I sat, I stared with a small glimmer in my eye at Jorge. I had seen that small smile he gave me in an earlier session. I was pretty sure he knew that I was an exception among the people here. So I gave him that glimmer, almost as if to share that secret.

But he didn't return that glimmer. He didn't return a smile or a wink or anything kind. He just looked deeply at me and said, "Irene, what makes you think anyone likes you?"

A double-take. Did he just ask why anyone liked me? I mean – I quivered – he wasn't going there was he? That had nothing to do with my therapy at Avalon. It had nothing to do with the things I'd written about. Why would he – I was sick inside – why would he ask something so stupid?

To make it all worse, hadn't I just written about a possible self-esteem issue? It had been haunting me for the past couple days because, as ridiculous as it was, something about it was eating at me inside. And now this. Now he asked why I thought anyone liked me. I was sick to my stomach and furious at the same time. It felt wrong. This was *not* what Avalon was supposed to be about, and I wouldn't put up with it. Truly. I stood and I began to walk out. "*Irene!*" yelled Jorge. I turned to face him with a challenge in my eye, but he stared right back and cut off my flight. "Sit down, Irene. We're just starting here." I swallowed. I was angry, confused, and concerned. I slowly sat again. I was hauntingly aware of all the eyes on me. I slowly sat down and looked at him again, no glimmer.

I closed my eyes and concentrated. Maybe I could meditate my way out of here – essentially just disappear. But when I opened my eyes, they were all still there, waiting. I opened my mouth to speak, but had to close it again and swallow once more. My throat was completely dry. I tried once more, and was surprised to hear myself squeak, "I'm co-dependent."

Good God! Had I said that? Had I said it out loud, while everyone was looking, listening, and judging? Had I . . . "What does that mean to you?" asked Jorge.

Another double-take. What kind of question was that? Jorge was a counselor. He knew damn well what co-dependence was. We had talked about it as one of the addictions here, a coping mechanism that you become addicted to as a means to avoid whatever you are trying to avoid. I felt the sweat on my forehead as it threatened to seep into my eyes. I wiped it away with my sleeve. I started thinking I would throw up, and I wondered if that would get me out of the Hot Seat. I gave it a minute, but nothing. Not quite sick enough. So I finally answered. "I do things to please others." There. Enough. I hated this. And even if I liked Jorge yesterday, I hated him today. I hated him now for making me say these stupid things, these embarrassing and invasive things in front of all the stupid strangers. What right did they have to listen in on something like this? It was even stupider because there was nothing wrong with me that they needed to fix here at Avalon. Just some silly questions about what to do with my personal relationship. My personal relationship, not to be made public.

Jorge and the counselors stared at me and I didn't know what else to say. Why didn't they let me go. Or ask another question. Or something. Enough with this silence. I looked out into the crowd and saw Jean. She was my only support. She knew I was desperate, and she offered one of her warm, reassuring smiles. I tried to breathe it in. Then I looked back at the counselors. "I don't get it. I've been here two weeks and I just don't get it," I told them quietly.

They looked at one another and Albert raised one eyebrow and asked, "What is 'it' Irene? What don't you get?"

I was suddenly livid and I stood from my seat and screamed, *"Why I'm here! I don't get why I'm fucking here!"* I was even appalled at myself as I heard the words spill out. I never used that word. But I was precisely that angry with them all.

Jorge looked at me sincerely and said, "I'm sorry Irene – could you use the microphone so everyone can hear you?"

I thought he had to be nuts, but as I gauged my situation, there I was still seated. I hadn't stood up. I hadn't yelled. I was so angry, it's what I felt and what I imagined, but in fact I had only whispered my comment. So I took hold of the microphone, I cleared my throat and I spoke with some control. "I came here because I wanted to make a decision about whether or not to stay with my marriage," I said. There it was all on the table. If someone wanted to judge me for that, let them. I was done playing around with this.

These people wouldn't see me again, except for Jean. I'd stop playing and I'd get through this and I'd be done with this stupid place for good.

"What is wrong with your marriage?" Martha asked.

"My husband and I live in the same house," I said. "but we live entirely separate lives. There's almost no communication. I don't get why we're together. It seems like there's no point, and I can't stand living without meaning. I'm not happy in the marriage and I wonder if I should stick it out."

"Is that how your parents live?" Jorge asked. "Living under the same roof but living miles apart?" I pause a moment, then I nod. "Well then you're just fucked up, aren't you? Go back to your seat."

What?!? Did he just say something so violent and vile about me and then dismiss me without a second thought? Did he just totally abuse me when I was more vulnerable than ever? The man was a bastard. I couldn't think of it in any other way. I steamed as I stood from the chair and I stormed to my seat. I didn't even look at Jean. I sat down in disgust and totally shut off. I didn't remember a single thing anyone said for the rest of the day.

Chapter Thirty-Four

I hated Avalon. I hated the counselors. I hated the sessions. And I hated that I dared to open my mouth on that Hot Seat. I should've just folded my arms and glared. And I hated that I knew that only on looking back. Plain to see and easy to say, I was set in a place of deep loathing and started bouncing back and forth between thoughts of just leaving the place, or not participating or, if they somehow kept me from either of those, just finishing myself off so they had no control left at all.

I sulked angrily in the first session of the next day, still not convinced what path I would take, when I suddenly saw that everything had changed. The Hot Seat was the end of our first two weeks, and from here on out, Jorge's wife Nichole would be our head counselor. Each of them had a distinct purpose. Jorge was there to help us see our problems and break us down – and boy did he accomplish that. Nichole was there for the rebuild, which she would do with love and total support. She walked in that first day with smiles and hugs for all and made us feel like cherished guests at Avalon, rather than the prisoners we'd been till that point. She handed out life-affirming quotes, was the answer to my prayers and perhaps the prayers of many other people in the room.

In the first two weeks, it had often been hard to ever see the wisdom of Jorge's ways because you spent most of the time wanting to slug him. Occasionally I appreciated what I thought he was doing but not often. With Nichole, I adored her from the start because she gave every reason to like her. I was actually willing to listen to her for my own sake, not for clients and not just to learn the language of Avalon, but because the Hot Seat pushed buttons so hurtful that I knew at last that something was wrong and I wanted to change before I left here. A tall order? Maybe yes. But I had two weeks and supposedly, they were masters of change here at Avalon.

So I listened as Nichole began with a talk about parents – a subject everyone was struggling with, I discovered. You could see that in both subtle and direct ways during the Hot Seat sessions. "We've all got it figured out now, haven't we?" Nichole asked us with sweetness dripping from her tongue. "Our parents did a lot to mess us up, didn't they? But by now, you also realize that you can't change anything that happened. You can only change your part in the equation. Our task now is to start looking at what changes each of you can make so it can get you on the path you've always wanted to be on.

"First things first, we've got to recognize a rather universal truth. Parents very seldom wake up one day and say, "I think I'd like to have kids so I can totally mess up their lives." No, parents generally have decent or at least more humane intentions. But the way they raise us is usually based deeply in the way they were raised and their parents learned from their parents before them and so on back down the ages. I can all but guarantee that those of you here with kids raised them the way your parents raised you even though you've been harboring this resentment against your parents and this notion that you would never screw up the way they did." I was pretty sure that Nichole was right. People usually did make that error. And while I knew that applied very little to me, even I would admit that I'd caught myself a few times thinking, *My God, I am my mother*. Luckily it was a once-in-a-blue-moon curse. "But we get to re-write the script," Nichole continued. "It's the beauty of each new generation. They get the choice to continue the pattern or start something brand new. Each of you will begin something new.

"There's another thing I'd like you to realize, because thinking of things this way often loosens up our opinions about our parents. We're so quick to demonize, even though they are largely victims the way we have been until now. Not only did your parents suffer at the hands of their own parents, but they also faced unique circumstances that put the pressure on in one way or another. They were too young when they married, or they were too old. They were too rich or too poor. They wanted a boy and got a girl. They lost a child. They wanted fewer children. They wanted more children. They didn't finish school because they had to support a family. They gave up a career they really wanted. They were physically or emotionally ill. They faced divorce or the death of loved ones in their lives. When pressure builds up, it needs to be released, and often parents release these things on their children. So your mother had to work and she made sure you knew every day what kind of sacrifice she was making for you and your father always said what kind of great man he would have been if he didn't have to spend his hours toiling for you. And by golly, what fantastic romance they could have kept between them if only they weren't pulling their hair out over the kids.

"As a result, you can never please them, can you? You've made their lives that difficult, so in turn, you'll do all you can to be the perfect child so they're not angry with you, and you set out on the impossible task of trying to please them no matter what, even though you are not the root cause of their unhappiness. See – you weren't the root cause, but you believed that you were, so as far as you knew, you should have been able to make the difference. But you couldn't. The unhappiness was all inside them, and if they had changed their own script, they could have found immense happiness in the very situation they were in.

"There are so many variations on the story," said Nichole. You could see the compassion in her eyes. She knew, deeply, what many of us had been through. It made me wonder what she'd experienced herself to have such sympathy for the rest of us – a sympathy you could practically feel seeping over you as you sat and listened to her. "There are so many variations, but they all go back to the fact of parents who were raised by imperfect parents, who didn't know how to change their own life scripts, who simply redirected the pressures that they themselves faced. But you needn't do the same. There are ways to absorb pressure and transmute it into something more, into something better. Then, as you pour it back into the world, you are pouring something beautiful instead of something hurtful, built on the pain you are feeling inside.

"You're going to learn how to do that over the next few days. We'll be role playing situations you faced in childhood. You'll learn how to transmute the pressures coming into your life. You'll learn how to view things differently and how to react differently. Before we begin, though, we'll do a bit more writing, because I want you to take some time reflecting on some of the issues involved. So you'll be looking over these sheets here," she said, picking some up from a desk, "and responding to each of the questions. I will see you this afternoon. You've got a few hours to go through this." With that, she bid us *adieu* and the counselors handed out the sheets. I took mine to my room and began sifting through the small pile of paper.

What kind of relationship did your mother have with her parents? How did this affect you? "Huh," I thought. Curious question. The next asked the same thing of my father. Others followed, including:

What kind of marriage do you think your parents had? If they fought, did you resent this? Did it scare you? Or were you used to breaking up their fights, or taking one side or the other? Or were they so close that you felt you couldn't be a part of them?

Were you wanted at birth? How old were you at the birth of your siblings? How did you feel about the new arrivals?

In general, describe what you think your family thought of you.

Did your appearance (looks, clothes, etc.) embarrass you? Did you feel that you were "different" form your classmates?

Any bad experiences with church or at Sunday school?

Were you afraid to fight?

How did your parents punish you? Did they try to reason, or was it physical? How did you react to this punishment?

There were dozens of questions like this and it was a little eerie – almost like they knew what to ask specifically because of my life story. But I wasn't so *naïve* as that; if they were asking these questions to all of us, then it was strangely true. We were all reacting to much the same kind of background, no matter the specific problems we faced today, which were just different ways of coping with the same crummy stuff.

I wrote and I wrote and I wrote. Amazing, I started to feel some relief spread across me as I did so. These were the right questions to ask and it felt good to answer them out loud, if only on paper. And it felt good, too, to know that I wasn't quite so alone as I had always believed. If we were all reacting to something similar – to poor parenting based on poor parenting, and pressures that our parents faced and didn't know how to change. I was not some lone freak passing through life without a person who could understand. If the people at Avalon could write these questions, maybe they could get me after all. And if everyone else was responding as I was to the questions, then maybe I wasn't so unlike them after all.

Chapter Thirty-Five

Over the next week and more, we spent time role-playing our childhoods, learning by reliving and by having the event mirrored to us in real time by objective adults. The people at the Center, and I don't just mean the counselors, often noticed things I never would have, because they stood outside. So often, they could relate because they were addicts in their own right, even if they were addicted to different things.

Learning through this process and seeing where we were wrong and deciding how we could improve, we developed our new life scripts – how we would view the world and react to things from now on. We again engaged in role playing to act out our new lifestyles and to cement them in our minds. A lot of times I felt badly for the others in the class, because I knew that I had developed a powerful new script for myself and I saw them struggling to create anything decent. Usually they developed something different from before, but powerful? No, not quite. But that was fine. Everyone had their own goals and ambitions in life, and mine were obviously farther-reaching than theirs.

My new role, in short, was not to judge, but also not to be judged. I would let others think of me what they wanted, but I would no longer react, because I would be focused on doing what I was here in this world to do. I had spent all my life reacting to my parents and then, after marriage, reacting to my husband. It meant that I was never taking an action of my own, because I was always responding to other people's actions. No more. Realistically, this meant that I could remain in my marriage and have a wholly new experience. But it also meant that, if I chose to get out for my own life purpose, I wouldn't give a damn what anyone thought of me. I hadn't yet decided which choice to make.

We were within days of going home when we finally came to relationships. We would write a script specifically for that and role play that with a classmate who would act as our relationship partner. Nichole and Wendy, another counselor there, sat with my partner and me and we began. We started with my classmate first and as we went through, I felt badly to see how she had limited herself in her script. She had not made herself as free as I had, and at one point, in her husband's place, I said, "Well that's fine, Rebecca. You're welcome to have Sunday evenings for your projects if that's what you need, but I feel the need to have the weeknights to myself, either at home or out with my buddies, I'm working too hard all day to feel that I should come home and take care of all your chores and the kids." She hadn't demanded much for herself because she was so used to bending to his every whim. I was showing her how much room he still had to give.

But Rebecca looked at me quizzically. "Sweetheart, I'm happy to give you some time for yourself. You earn it. But we need you at home, too, if we're going to call ourselves a family."

"Hey, if I'm providing for you guys, that makes us a family," I said craftily. "We sleep in the same bed every night and I'll be with the kids every night. You want to pressure me right out of the marriage with more?"

"Ok, that's enough," said Wendy. "I think you've done a wonderful job, Rebecca, of moving things forward by sharing your needs and finding a way to have your husband help you." She looked at me. "Irene, I'm not sure why you think she should change things overnight. One step at a time. Remember, we've talked about this."

I shrugged. "Ok. I just think she could talk about more needs than that. Otherwise her husband's going to get just one piece at a time and he'll feel like things are always changing in the wrong direction — always more and more for her. Might as well get it all out on the table and then just implement one thing at a time at a pace that's good for everyone."

"Hmm ..." said Nichole. "Seems like that would put more pressure on the poor guy in two seconds than her approach. Remember, this isn't about coming up with everything that's wrong in your life and fixing it overnight. It's about responding to things in a new way and I think, Rebecca," she said, looking back at my classmate, "that you did a very nice job with that. Let's go on to Irene's role play."

Boy was I ready for this. Seemed like I was waiting through all of Avalon for this one moment. We started with small talk and then I launched in. "Honey, I've got some exciting news. I'm going to stop with my career-development coaching and my massage and I'm going to focus on something that's been building in me for a long time. I'm going to write a book."

"A book? That's terrific Honey," said Rebecca. "But won't that put a lot of financial pressure on us when you drop both of your jobs?"

"That's how it always is, though, Bob, isn't it? We're always worried about financial pressures rather than on what is most important to us, aren't we?"

"Gosh, Irene — seems like paying the bills has always been important to us. We're going to have to cut back on a *lot* of the things we enjoy if we suddenly don't have that money."

"But we'll manage Bob. We've always managed, no matter what our income. We're making so much more now than we ever used to, so how come we don't have enough in savings for me to take this time off? We'll cut back and we'll manage, because writing this book is why I'm here Bob. I've been through it all, the kind of stuff a lot of people go through, and that other people are putting their kids and loved ones through. And I, for one, would like to offer some insights to help let people see their experiences as common and forgivable, to offer advice to others who are still raising their kids so they don't make the same mistakes their parents made. Teaching. Healing. That's why I'm here – not for the things you think we enjoy. I can never enjoy those as much as you think, because I am frankly not fulfilled. I can't take no for an answer on this one, Bob. I can't take no for an answer."

Rebecca held up her hands in mock surrender. "That's ok!" she exclaimed. "I wasn't giving you a no. Just pointing out the kind of pinch it'll put us into."

"Don't you think that's a way to manipulate my choices though?" I asked. "Put on the subtle guilt trip so that I end up agreeing we have to bow to financial pressures?"

Rebecca furrowed her brow. "No," she said flatly. And I could hear Bob in her voice. "I'm pointing out the obvious to make sure you know what we will face and so that we can make a conscious choice together about it."

"There's not really a choice to make," I responded. "It must be, or else my life here is without worth, which means this marriage is without worth."

"Whoa ho ho!" said Nichole, stopping my momentum. "Irene, you have gone into this with an agenda. You've gone in with your mind set about the meaning behind everything your husband says. You've gone in deciding that you will be right and your husband will be wrong, and that this, in turn, will help you put pressure on the marriage and that you can fault him for it. Well enough of this! I thought you were finally getting what we're doing here, but you're not. You're way out in left field. You're not creating a new response. You are just demonizing your husband before things have even begun. You're demonizing Rebecca's new script in her marriage. It's exactly what I've seen this entire week and a half. You're just a demanding bitch! No one else is as good as you. You're the best, aren't you? Well that's not the kind of person we try to help you to be here and I can't let this go on. You're done in this room until you've got a new script. A valuable script. One that responds in a positive way to life – not one that wants to control life at all costs. You never gave up that control, did you? Well, you've got to now or your time here will have been an entire waste. You got that? Go on and write that script again. I'm going to be here when you're done and you'd better impress the hell out of me."

My mouth was literally hanging wide. This was *Nichole* – sweet, gentle Nichole. Where did this inner witch crawl from? I glared at her, incredulous. "It's already been a waste of my time," I glowered. "You're going to tell me that I finally stand in a place of power after all these years and suddenly I'm too demanding. Well screw that! You guys can't make up your minds. I don't have to impress you. I just have to wait out my last couple days and get the hell out of here, forever."

"Suit your highfalutin' self," said Nichole. "You want our help, I'm here. But until you're ready with something that respects other people, get the hell out of my sight."

I shook my head and stood, steaming. What a damn crock this was! She had played nice girl for ten days, only to come in and destroy me at the very end. They were toying with people here. I could see that now. Destroy them, pick them up and dust them off so they love you, destroy them again, and pick them up again. Keep it up, and you'd have an army of morons who all thought you were god. A cult. That's what this was. And Jorge and Nichole were the godheads. I stormed from the room, wondering what I was going to do from this point on here at Avalon. Where was Jean? I needed to talk with her and she'd been in a different group for role playing. I had to find her. She would be the only one with an answer that made some sense … if anyone could come up with a sensible answer about a cult.

I headed out on a two-hour walk through the woods of Avalon, consumed by what happened the entire time, I came back more emotional than when I left. I had thoughts of suing the place for emotional abuse. This was not a legitimate therapy and I couldn't let other people suffer through it the way I had. I knew my lawyer would agree.

When I walked back into the lounge, Jean was there. She saw me and knew instantly that something was drastically wrong. She approached me and I stood, trying only not to cry. "What is it?" she asked. "What happened." I blinked. Every effort went to not crying. I shrugged and my mouth quivered a little. I walked past her with an understood invitation for her to follow. She did so, walking into my room behind me and closing the door. I turned and looked at her for as long as I could, surely less than thirty seconds, but feeling that it was much longer, and that was it. There was no strength left. I broke into tears and the flow began like none I had ever known. I cried loudly, unashamed, and before long, Jean was crying with me. We embraced, and the tears rolled on and on, an anguish and a relief all at once. The stress of my life seemed to be passing over me and over me and there was no way to stop it. It had to wash itself clean through my tears.

The two of us fell onto the bed, a heap of shaking and tears. Fifteen minutes, nothing but wailing and then, as the last of the pain swept across me, something burst inside me – an awareness like nothing I'd ever known. Relief. I had totally lost control, and it felt as though God took my every burden onto Himself. In that moment, I felt light and I started to laugh right through my tears. Somehow, in that moment, I experienced gratitude and joy in a way that only those who experience it will ever know. It is not something that can be expressed in words and anyone who has known bliss would laugh at me for trying. Bliss – that was the word. I was absolutely in the sweet spot of life.

As I began to laugh, I looked at Jean, and she began to smile too. "I get it," I told her. "I finally get it!"

She laughed. "I get it too – like I never have before!"

God had somehow stepped in. He lifted the veil for us to look beyond and see what it was all most truly about. I could only feel love. In fact, it seemed that I *was* love, and that nothing else – at *all* – mattered. I was completely absorbed and my body shook. It could not handle the power that was suddenly my only reality. So great was the relief, it could only be compared to a cool shower after a day in the desert sun. It minimized and yet made more spectacular each one of life's smallest pleasures, birds singing in the morning, a fire roaring in the winter, the blaze of autumn leaves, the gurgling of a brook. It was all of these things at once. It was infinitely more. Jean and I lay on the bed for an hour or more, absorbing it all. And at last, when we calmed just a little, I told her I had work to do. I had a script to write. I had a new response to life, and at last, my big ego would not write the script. Love would write my script and I knew that from then on things were going to be okay.

Chapter Thirty-Six

The script I wrote for myself was unlike anything I had come up with till then, because it came from completely a new way of looking at things. I had never experienced life purely from a place of love, and while I wrote, that was the place I was in. It was an experience of the soul and I believe that for the most part those experiences are short-lived. The human body is too fragile to handle that kind of power for long. But it gives you a glimpse of the goal and the way to that goal. The script I wrote would be that way, leading eventually to more and more responses from honest love.

When I presented the new script in role playing, Nichole looked at me and shook her head. But I knew that was a good thing right away, because her eyes were welling up. "Now that is a script for life," she told me; and she touched me gently on the shoulder. "There is awakening after all, isn't there?" she asked. And I nodded my head.

I had awakened to the fact that my husband had not spent all these years deciding that I must be kept at all costs from fulfillment any more than I had decided the same thing for him. He simply viewed things from a practical standpoint and I couldn't argue with the fact that he lived in a way that got the bills paid and that helped us raise our kids with a modicum of success. For all I knew, everything we had done could have pleased him, or he could have set his dreams aside long ago, believing that he had a duty to fulfill supporting us, and he would do so at all costs. All along I had thought only of my own dreams. My intuition told me I hadn't yet filled my purpose and the practical life that Bob insisted on for us was what I blamed it on.

Maybe. But our practical life was not to keep me from my destiny, but to support the family we had decided on together. It honestly seemed the right thing for Bob. And what had I done? I had bowed to his every whim rather than going where my intuition led. Why? Because I had spent my entire childhood bowing to the whims of someone else. It was all I had learned. It was all I knew to carry into marriage. I was there to serve my husband, because I had no model for teaming-up, the way a married couple is meant to, and I had no idea how to be an independent person.

The new script was based on the wisdom I had found in the moment of love. Bowing to others failed to honor my own worth. Asking others to bow to me failed to honor theirs. It was only by removing personal judgments and respecting that the other person was expressing themselves in the only way they could – maybe because of the kinds of challenges as I had faced – only in loving them for who they were and responding accordingly would my needs and theirs be met. As I worked my way through this script and had

Nichole's tender approval after her zeal of the other day, I knew at last that my time here was wrapping up, and that I *had* found the kind of success this place was famous for.

On the final day before our families arrived, we had what was called a "Wonder Child" ceremony. We would choose a classmate, and each would personify the other the beauty inside us that had made its way out, the glory that lived inside, but that could dwell in everything we did if we wished. Of course I selected Jean as my Wonder Child, and it was among the most deeply moving events of my life. I stood in a white robe in the midst of all my classmates and their attention. But this was no Hot Seat. This time, I was the star attraction, not to be ridiculed, but to be honored. Jean walked up beside me, she read for me what she felt my Wonder Child had to tell me:

My name is Irene Watson. I am your Wonder Child. I am your uniqueness. I am the vibrant, awake, and loving woman in you. I am the purity of your being, and the essence of God's spirit expressing as you, Irene. I am whole, free, and my nature is sacred.

I am the wellspring of joy that emanates from the core of your soul. I am the peaceful one in you who understands and values inner silence. I am the one who listens to the still, small voice and quietly obeys. I am the healer in you.

I am the creative and dependable one who is also capable of discipline and follow through. I am the loyal, trusting, and willing one who sees others through the eyes of identity without judgment or blame. I am the intuitive one who has clarity and purity of intent.

I am the one who understands that recovery is a conscious choice, and I freely choose it. I am the decisive one, the appreciative one who has a heart full of gratitude and forgiveness. I am your burning desire to express more of the beauty, goodness, and genius that lies within your being.

I have never abandoned you, Irene. In hardships, difficulties, emptiness, codependency, fear, rejections, and spiritual darkness, I was there. My love for you never diminished or lessened. You are most valuable and deserving. I approve of you. I respect the glorious being of light that you are. I am your triumphant, surviving power. Your victories over ego are wondrous to see. You are a blessing and most valued. I love you. I am you. And we are one.

Welcome home, my dearest Friend.

○

Our ceremonies and dinner that day came to a close, and the next day families would begin to arrive for two final days, during which they would learn about what we had gone through in our twenty eight days and what they could expect on our return home. It was like an orientation to the new family members they now had.

My experience of deep love had passed, but it was still vivid in my mind. I knew how I was meant to be with Bob now. I knew how I wanted to be. And yet, without the support of that very definite soul contact, I was left to my own, human emotions once more, and I didn't know how I actually would respond to seeing him. Would I see the beauty in him? The goodness? The man who had most likely sacrificed much of what he wanted in this world in order to be with me? Would I see the man whose staunch, practical nature had kept me from risks I felt I should take in order to fulfill my purpose? Or would I see and feel something else?

This was my husband of so many years, and this first reaction would perhaps drive my decisions, sill not concrete in my mind, of whether I would remain in that marriage. My script called for honoring him for all that he was, for respecting and loving him and for bringing forth my own needs within our relationship. But my script did not rely on him responding well. If he did not, there was nothing to keep me from dissolving our marriage. And that was an absolutely frightening thought. I had been married since I was twenty one years old.

I sat on a picnic bench, waiting for the van that would bring many of our family members from the airport. Detached. It was like I was looking from outside myself, utterly curious about what would happen next, but without emotion. And yet, inside my body, I felt a growing anxiety. It was a strange sensation, experiencing fear and watching myself being afraid in the same moment.

The white van drove up, and family members poured out. There was Bob in their midst. I didn't move, even to wave him over. I would let him see me and come over. It wasn't meant as a power play. It was as if time would bring us together, and I would let it. I wasn't in a rush. I didn't need to avoid. When he saw me and waved, my heart skipped once – that curious anxiety inside the calm. I smiled, peacefully and stood from the table. We walked toward one another. And suddenly, the anxiety floated. Just floated off. Because that singular sensation of love, of soul contact, swept in once more to remind me how things were. I experienced the meaning of my script again. And in that moment, I knew that I would always be with Bob. I also knew that, as my needs were expressed, he would support them as far as he could. That was enough to let me feel deep love for someone I thought I had lost my love for, when in fact, I had buried the love inside myself, because that was how I coped. That was how I learned to cope. But no more. Life was something fresh now. Something new. I had escaped the patterns I learned as a child, and now I would be an adult, loving another adult, and sharing support with him for many years to come.

○

There was, then, one last event and one last person to come to terms with. The next night, before we left, we would close our time together by releasing that which we had found in ourselves and no longer had a use for. The old self that had responded to life in one way, and now that we'd found healthier ways to respond, that old self could be put to rest. We had each written out a good deal about that old self over the last many days. Now, we were receiving all of this writing in sealed envelopes from Jorge himself. We were to burn the envelope, setting that old way of life free.

As my name was called, I took my husband's hand and walked proudly up onto the stage. Yes, proudly. Kicking and screaming, I'd been dragged through the twenty eight days, set against learning, certain that they could teach nothing of much use. But now I was proud, because I saw a new me taking flight already. We took the stage and approached Jorge. Inside, my new script scrambled to find peace with the man who had emotionally abused me so badly. I smiled, but weakly, at Jorge. It was the best I could muster. I told myself over and over that, for whatever reason, he had felt the need to be harsh with me. All I had to do now was feel grateful that all had ended well, and I would never again see his face. I only prayed that he would be less harsh with others in the future.

Now, before Jorge, I stood courageously and he handed me my envelope. "Yours to burn. Yours to let go of," he told me. He shook Bob's hand, then faced me again and gave me a wink. My heart skipped once more. Was this some sign? Some sign of recognition that all we had been through together was no more than a play? He leaned in close to me and whispered: "By the way, we do like you. We like you a lot. You're one of the very special few, and you just had to find that out about yourself. Burn this envelope. That was a lifetime ago."

Shivers raced through me. Truth! What he said was a deep and lasting truth, he had looked beyond the surface. He had pushed me, harder than he had pushed some, because he really did care. As the shivers took me, he smiled, then hugged me as few could do – the hug that you know lasts forever, because it is between spiritual friends. Only a spiritual friend could do what Jorge had done. He had broken my ego into pieces, giving my soul the chance to take over and create a new life that would give me meaning and the chance, at last, to fulfill my purpose for being alive.

Chapter Thirty-Seven

Several years after Avalon Bob and I received an invitation to our high school reunion. Though Bob was a few years older, reunions were always open to everyone who'd attended during the time the school was a high school. It only made sense with such a small number of students. We hadn't been to a reunion in twenty years; hadn't seen our hometown in ten. In particular, had never stopped in since my stay at Avalon. It was time.

We flew in one evening and took our rental car into the sleepy town, cruising the few streets and the roads out to the farms, reminiscing our lives there. There was something special about a small community. It was a blessing and curse all at once: everyone knew everyone, and everyone knew what everyone else was doing. So there was support, and there was nosiness. But for raising a family, there was value in knowing the world around you so intimately.

Still, the place didn't fit us at all anymore. Our horizons were distant. Visiting here felt like a trip into past lives for us both, and we knew it was good for us now only as a reflection of where we had been and a context for where we were now.

My uncle, the one who was thunder and lightning as a Baptist preacher, knew I was coming into town, so our first visit was with him and my aunt. I had come to terms with so much that was my childhood, but I wanted to know about my brother. It seemed enough time had passed for the question to be asked. So I addressed my uncle, wondering aloud just what had happened that my brother had died as an infant.

My uncle furrowed his brow. "Oh, those are days long past. No use in talking about them."

"It can't hurt," I assured him. "I'm just curious to understand that piece of my childhood."

My uncle looked directly at me and spoke solemnly. "Long time ago, and best to leave it alone. Enough to say, your mother didn't kill the baby." The comment was so enigmatic that it startled me, and I tried to pursue it. "Long time ago," my uncle said once more. And then he wouldn't say a word about it.

After our visit with them, Bob and I headed to see my other cousins – the ones who had taunted me throughout my childhood. My aunt had moved to another home and the cousins were there with their spouses for the reunion. What a difference it makes when people have matured! Old rivalries become as nothing in the face of time if people will only grow up. My cousins never had a thing against me but, like all of us, had their own personal issues to struggle through and my unfortunate years had been one of their outlets. Now, they had struggled and had found their way. Now, there was conversation and laughter and pictures. When I left that day, most of that pain was gone for me.

There was only one thing more I needed to do about my cousins, and that night at the reunion, I followed through. I found the one cousin older than me who I should have been able to count on for support when I had no friends in school, the one who, in the end, spent more time harassing me than anyone. I approached him that night and went through it all in a moment, reminding him off the beatings and the shame and the frustration and the fear. He nodded his head throughout my tales. "But I forgive you," I told him at last. "You did all these things to me, but I've had years now to look at it. Today, I know that your abuse helped me to become stronger, and helped me to stand up for myself in the long run. There is no forgiving abuse, ever. But I can forgive you, as a person, and I do." He was still just nodding his head when I turned calmly away and left. There was no malice in what I said. I was only addressing it, closing it. And my cousin let me do just that.

Margie was in town too, of course. I hadn't seen her since the last reunion I attended, and we became like teens again when we met. The next day, Bob and I took up her invitation to come by her parents' home to see the place, and I just shook my head. Exactly the same. Exactly. Oh, some of the bushes were a little more grown in, but the house was kept up just as it had always been. Furniture, decorations, all the same. Bob stayed downstairs and talked with Margie's parents while Margie and I headed into her old bedroom, which itself was left largely untouched over the years. We plopped onto the bed and shared girl talk for a long time.

Still another stop or two for my sake, and the next was the most sobering of the trip. I'd solved plenty inside myself surrounding my childhood. I wasn't afraid to face it anymore, and I felt it was important to go back to the two-room house where I believed that Mom was my world, and where I'd spent days upon days resting motionless on the sitting swing.

Strangely enough, Margie's brother now owned the land. You could see where most of the old buildings once stood, pride of a man's hard work. The house still stood and I pushed my way through the tall, waving grasses to get to it.

I could almost hear my mother telling me that I'd planted the flowers badly and that she would have to redo the job. I could hear her asking me to stand back and just stay clear. I was ok with that now. It was a poor thing to do to a child, a poor way to include and teach her. But it no longer riled me. It was not something that could be changed, at least between my mother and me. But it was a lesson for the rest of us, I felt. A child needs so much more if we want her to grow into her potential.

As I approached the badly worn front porch, I began feeling nervous about what I would see inside and how I would react. Was there anything still in me not yet solved? Would I trigger some unremembered event? I slowed my pace and Bob, who'd been plodding quietly behind me, stepped by me and pushed open the old door. He pushed back the cobwebs and some fallen boards and gestured for me to join him. Timidly, I did.

The world rushed back on me. I could see the counter where my mom used to keep the so-called sink. I saw where the stove once stood, and the cupboard, and the couch where I'd been beaten. I could imagine in detail where we used to eat dinner, and where Mom and Dad would fight unless I was in trouble and they were acting more as a team. I even saw the window, long since broken out, through which Mom used to watch me sitting motionless on the swing. I know it's common to go back and look at our childhood world and discover with surprise how small it really was. But this? This was extraordinary. It seemed that Bob and I filled the whole room, yet I remembered distinctly how we used to have family and friends over, and everyone had room to gather. Strange to think how full it must have been with furniture and people, but that was that. Things are very different indeed when your perspective changes. Today we demand space and more space. For me, it had once been enough to have a place to eat and sleep.

Bob was silent as I soaked it in and experienced what was there. And strangely, a calm swept across me, and a very distinct sensation of gratitude. I knew, now, where I came from, and I understood how it had bent me, shaped me, into who I was today. Not a day goes by when I'm not looking for ways to improve; but I was glad for what I had achieved to that point, and no matter what, this house was part of that achievement.

The story of my life played through one more time as we stood there those few minutes, but unlike the experience at Avalon, this time around it was settling and satisfying. When I walked out of the house with Bob, I knew that it was all inside me now as a lesson, and never again as a nightmare. I looked back at the house one more time and nodded. Yes, the old place had a beauty in an unpretentious way. Now I could look forward, and I did. We got into the car, drove off, and I never looked back again.

Closed. It was all but closed now, and I was ready to head home and into my new world and life of applying my lessons and sharing them with others. But there was still one good-bye that I felt was important. There was one person who'd had perhaps more influence on me than any other, perhaps more than my mother. And sad to say, I'd never really known him.

Bob and I pulled into the small-town cemetery and, as if by instinct, I knew where to go and find one tiny gravestone: *Alexander Novak – October 6, 1942 to December 18, 1942.* In spite of my uncle's words, I couldn't help but keep wondering what really had happened. What was the lesson for my parents? What was the lesson for me?

I stooped down beside the stone and quietly spoke, the only words I ever shared with my brother. "Thank you, Alexander," I told him. "I don't know how things would have been different if you'd lived longer. Maybe I'd have had more freedom. Maybe I'd have had more friends and someone to defend me against my cousins. But there's no second-guessing things, is there? If you hadn't been born, things would have been different. If you had lived longer, things would have been different. But who knows if they'd have been better or worse. I am who I am today because you were born and stayed just a little while. That was your path and this is mine. So thank you, Alexander," I said once more. I patted the stone and stood, and with one deep breath, I turned, took my husband's hand, and made my way from the cemetery, my brother's gravestone disappearing behind me forever.

About the Author

Irene Watson has designed and facilitated workshops and retreats throughout the United States and Canada. She received her Master of Arts, with honors, in Psychology, from Regis University in Denver. Her emphasis was in spirituality and psychosynthesis. She is listed in *Who's Who of American Women 2004- 2005*; is author of the poem *Gifts* published by *The National Library of Poetry* in 1996. She lives with her husband in Austin, Texas.

Printed in the United States
35949LVS00006B/173-222